How to be a Great Employee

(and a Greater Manager)

By Robert Villegas

How to be a Great Employee (and a Greater Manager)
By Robert Villegas

© Copyright 2017 by Robert Villegas. All Rights Reserved. No part of this book may be reproduced in any manner without written permission from the copyright holder or his legal representative/s.

ISBN-13: 978-1977907219

ISBN-10: 1977907210

Series Title: Villegas Business Volume 1

www.robertvillegas.com

Published by Robert Villegas

Email the author: robertv1989@outlook.com

Table of Contents

INTRODUCTION 6
YOU HAVE A JOB.. 8
HOW TO SURVIVE... 14
WHAT IS PRODUCTION?... 20
THE VALUE OF A GOOD ATTITUDE 25
HOW TO MANAGE YOUR ATTITUDE................................ 32
THE HINES STORY 55
MANAGEMENT BY WALKING AROUND 61
MANAGEMENT BY OBJECTIVES.. 64
DO NOT BE A MARXIST... 65
JOHN PAUL GETTY – THE THREE RULES TO RICHES.. 69
DISCOVERING CONCEPTS AND HOW TO USE THEM IN BUSINESS 73
FREE WILL 80
HOW TO THINK 82
THE IMPORTANCE OF FOCUS 84
LOGIC.. 86
CAUSE AND EFFECT 89
FORMS OF THE LOGICAL THINKING............... 91
Induction 94
Deduction... 97
LOGICAL FALLACIES 101
DECISION-MAKING 110
DECISION-MAKING WORKSHEET.................................... 111
PROBLEM SOLVING.. 114
Problem Solving Worksheet 116
PRAGMATISM 120
GENERATING NEW IDEAS 124

HOW IS YOUR VOCABULARY? 133
DEALING WITH CONFLICT AT WORK 135
A Boss You Do Not Like.. 136
How to Get Your Boss on Your Side 138
Conflict with the Boss 140
Gossip 143
INSPIRATION 144

Dedicated to

Roberto Villegas III

A Great Employee

And

A Greater Manager

Introduction

You have purchased this book because you want to be a better employee. Or someone has given you this book because they thought you might benefit from the principles it teaches.

Great bosses and managers start out as great employees. In fact, it is as employees that they demonstrated their management abilities. They realized that when they benefited their company and its customers, they proved their worth. There is no getting around it.

This book is based on my years of management experience as well as my years as an "employee". I started my work career in the Army as a private. I served in Korea during the 1960s. Later, I spent 27 years at United Parcel Service and eventually became a manager running my own department. I even travelled throughout Europe for UPS installing computer systems for call centers in Germany, England, Singapore, and Spain. I designed computer software that saved UPS millions of dollars and I was rewarded for my efforts.

Yes, I was once a young man who had to make his own way in the world. Like you, I had to learn to survive. And that is where we begin this book.

You have a Job

First, we'll assume that you have a job and that you want to get beyond this job to bigger and better things. You want to climb the ladder of success, so to speak. But you don't know where to start because this seems like such an unimportant job, entry-level and, well, you feel like a freshman in high school again. What's next?

The fundamental truth is that you cannot be a great manager or business owner without first being a great employee. And this is something that requires learning, experience, and attitude. The attitude comes from you but the learning and experience you should acquire through diligent study and practice. Everything you do as an employee must be looked at as preparation for management and the more you apply yourself to that preparation, the sooner you will be able to bridge the gap between being an employee and being a business owner or manager.

A good place to start is by finding out some important things:

Who is the business owner?

How did he start the business?

What does the business do?

What are the company mission and vision statements?

How does your boss work? Is he or she a doer or a delegator?

What is the boss's work day like?

How does he or she treat the people who work for him?

Is he or she easy to approach or is he a long-distance manager who works through subordinate managers?

What are his goals for him- or herself?

What are his goals for the company?

How does he discipline errant employees?

There are, of course, some simple matters to which you should attend. The first is getting along with people. You'll never be successful if you can't take simple instructions from your boss and "do it". You'll also need to be proficient at using the spoken word to communicate with other people. This isn't something you just "get"; you should study English communication and English grammar for starters. If you didn't go to a school that emphasized these skills, you can enroll in a college course or free course of some type. However, this isn't something that you can simply ignore. It is critical to your success.

In the meantime, you must also work on convincing your boss that you bring value to the company. Simply put, if he doesn't make money from your work, if he doesn't get back from you the money he spends on you, well then, you aren't worth much. So, you need to address your job requirements with full focus and ensure that you do your job to the best of your ability. You cannot get around this issue.

For the future, it would be a good idea to look at the skills you will need for the jobs that are higher up on the ladder of your success. Look at these positions in the company and determine if you need to develop new skills which you presently do not have and schedule some time to take classes, read books, etc. so that you know those skills.

It does you no good to have a conflict with your boss if you aren't first doing your job with skill and diligence. If you can't be productive, if you can't give value, then it is not his responsibility to give you more money than you are worth. This is a simple fact of reality. Forget about the ideology of social justice. If you can't perform your work, ideology means nothing. Why burden your boss with the chore of having to be fair to you when you are not being fair to him through your productivity?

Of course, your boss will never tell you this. In fact, I've never heard a boss of mine tell me this important simple fact. You must work and you must produce, or you will not be able to feed, house and clothe your family.

The principle that works best in business is "value for value", mutual trade to mutual benefit. You must do everything you can to bring value to your company or boss; and you must do it fairly and honestly by knowing what your boss expects and doing it to perfection. This is not too much to expect.

To give an example, I once had a job as a marketing manager for my company. I saw that my company was struggling to get new business, so I took it upon myself (on my own time) to do some research. I found that there was an online source of information about available projects for which my company could apply. Asking a few questions around work, I discovered that my senior management had no idea about this source. There was an opportunity here. I began to look through this source and discovered that a local company was beginning to take up a project to use railroad easements to offer fiber optic and cable communications. I forwarded this information to my immediate manager and within a few weeks the company signed a $9,000,000.00 contract to develop this property. That's how to bring value (and it helped me get a raise). Afterwards, my research became part of my daily job and I was allowed to send what I uncovered directly to the company CEO. That got me noticed.

So, having a job is more than just punching a clock. It is more than just doing a mundane activity exactly as it is supposed to be done (although sometimes this is a value too); having a job is about bringing value to your company and the more value you bring, the more critical you are to the company's success, and the more money you will make and the sooner you will be promoted and be able to buy a nicer house for your family. You see, it is not about telling your boss to take his job and shove it. That job is a goldmine, and you should treasure it. Change your attitude and you'll change your life.

How to Survive

As a child, you survive by the work of your parents or caretakers. They provide you with the food, clothing and shelter that will keep you alive, healthy, and secure. You survive because they love you. The more successful they are, the more resources they can bring to the task of raising you well.

But had you never been born; your parents would still have needed to survive. They would have had to take actions that led to their securing food, clothing, and shelter. Whether they were working to exchange money with an employer or living on their own in the wilderness, they would have had to engage in some type of action that led to survival.

Survival is not accomplished in a vacuum. You *must* identify your needs by looking at reality and choosing the values that you will pursue, then you *must* take direct action to accomplish them. The more assertive and/or aggressive you are at taking these actions, the better for your survival. This starts by recognizing what you need to survive and, as we discussed above, taking some sort of action. If you live alone on a desert island, then you must produce these values for yourself. If you live in an advanced society, you can decide on a good specialization and trade what you produce with others who have their own specializations.

Over many thousands of years, men have created a variety of tools to make survival easier. Early on, someone invented stone tools for striking other things into desired shapes. These tools helped man obtain food, make his own clothing, and build his own shelters. In modern times, man has taken the primitive forms of food, shelter and clothing and automated the processes to such a degree that few people are required to make their own food, homes, and clothes. This is advanced society, and it makes life easier.

One of the most important institutions in advanced society is the phenomenon of capitalism. Capitalism is a way of organizing society around a specific principle which we call "individual rights". Every individual has the freedom and the responsibility to create his own survival according to the free use of his mind, according to reason. This is what makes capitalism such an efficient system. The combination of millions of people each using their minds to make the right decisions about what they want creates an efficient mechanism where demand is met by supply, and everyone is benefited. The profit motive is the principle that makes capitalism efficient compared to socialism which violates supply and demand (as well as individual rights) continuously.

Yet, capitalism is also attacked and criticized today. Karl Marx, the famous anti-capitalist, was only the beginning. Before Marx (who lived during the 1800s), many religions denigrated the practices of usury and commerce as evil. They were thought to be forms of theft and anyone who made a profit was considered ungodly and malicious.

I disagree with the anti-capitalist viewpoint. In my view, capitalism is the most efficient system in history especially when it comes to alleviating poverty and giving people a chance to survive well. If people want to have a bright future, then it is only capitalism that will bring it.

Capitalism is good and if you disagree, try living in a socialist or communist country. You'll see that socialism or communism are poorly functioning systems that create poverty. Socialism or communism are based upon the idea of coercive management of the economy by the government. There is no freedom there; there is no possibility of good if the government is constantly taking from the productive.

The question about whether capitalism is good or not *is* an important one. Why work in a system that you think exploits you? Why exploit others when the solution to human problems is production and trade? Should an evil system be abolished? What would be the result of abolishing capitalism?

At some point, if you are to be successful at

surviving, you will have to decide whether capitalism is good or evil. I think that all evidence points to the truth that free people deciding for themselves will always be able to create affluence for themselves, and, on a wider scale, in society.

When we come to the issue of how you can survive, here are the essential principles that you must accept if you are to survive in a capitalist system:

1. Survival requires production – the more production you accomplish, the better the survival; likewise, the better the product, the better the survival
2. Survival requires law and order in society – good laws provide stability and enable production through the years
3. Survival requires individual liberty – individual liberty means better decisions by individuals which means better production
4. Survival requires moral living – morality means using your mind to decide correct

action – the better the choices, the higher the morality
5. Survival requires independent thinking – independence means relying on your own mind first which leads to better decisions
6. Survival requires the freedom of speech – freedom of speech means freedom of the mind

What is Production?

Production is the act of making or creating the tools of survival and other values that enhance life. In order to produce, you must succeed in using your mind, your hands and your thinking to make the values that will benefit your life through trade with other human beings. The key here is to recognize that the more values you produce, the more value you are selling to your customers. A whole society of people dedicated to creating values benefits not only your life and those of your loved ones, but also the lives of your customers. Because capitalistic society protects people from violence and fraud, more members of society are able to focus on morality; on creating values. This benefits everyone.

When you work in a factory, you are being productive to the extent to which you supply or exceed your boss's requirements. To the extent that you fall short of his requirements, you are draining capital from his bottom line. In this case, you must either improve your production or lose your job.

How does your boss create the conditions through which you are able to be productive? He does it by first identifying a product that will meet the needs of customers. Then he will learn about the tools and methods that will make the product. Then he invests money in factory and equipment designed to make that product. Then he invests in payroll to train you on how to use this equipment, produce the product, ship it, and sell it to customers who will pay him more than his investments. You, as a producer, are part of this process and if you do your job properly, you should be proud of your accomplishments. You will collect a paycheck, put money in the bank, buy the things you need for survival and enjoy a good life in a good home for your family.

This "social" approach to survival is far superior to the "desert island" approach in which you produce what you need to survive by yourself. Living in society can be a great benefit for you. All you need to do is hone your skills to the highest level and make monetary rewards by trading your labor or products with others.

In both cases (social and desert island), it is the efficient use of the human mind that is central to survival. Yet, an advanced society makes it possible for you to create more abundance because it allows for cooperation among people with high skills. This allows for specialization which enables better products and services. Specialization is the key to an ever-improving society as products get better and better and prices for "necessities" progressively drop.

I consider the "survivalist" (wilderness) approach to be flawed for the following reasons:

1. The survivalist eschews advanced society as artificial, robotic, and meaningless which is essentially a bias.
2. This view eschews organized society and extols the virtues of a life lived in the wilderness, but it relies on machines made in society.
3. It extols the virtues of lower forms of technology which means lower forms of thought.

4. It opposes capitalism in favor of barter which is a more primitive and less efficient trading system.
5. It advances a whim-based morality where men live without reason and good judgment.

A key flaw with survivalism is item #2 above; that it relies on capitalism for some of its tools. Manufacturers of food, guns, knives, etc. provide survivalists with better survival opportunities in the wild. They also use generators, automobiles, and other technologies to espouse a life in the wilderness.

In my view, the true survivalists are people who accept and exploit the benefits of capitalism and practice the morality of self-interest. In advanced society, the benefits of supply and demand, economic liberty, law and order and individual rights make survival truly possible. This is where an individual like you, seeking the best in life, can truly flourish.

Now that we've established that production is

necessary for survival, we will identify some of the key concepts that significantly affect your success in society.

The Value of a Good Attitude

An attitude is "(a) manner of thinking, feeling, or behaving that reflects a particular state of mind or disposition."[1]

Attitude is a component of your personality. It can be permanent, transitioning, or frequently changing depending upon the individual's state of mind at any particular time. Attitude can be contextual or general and most people have different attitudes in different contexts, and, at the same time, they can have a generalized attitude that is brought into every context in which they live or work.

What is the value of having a good attitude; and what is the value of it? How can you control and manage one's attitude? How does one control the influence of emotions on attitude? Which comes first, attitude or happiness?

---

[1] The American Heritage® Dictionary of the English Language, 5th Edition.

The normal condition of life should be a state of happiness. Even goal-directed action has the implicit goal of happiness. It is normal to be happy while one is working. Sadness, on the other hand, being the exception, is not the normal state. Anyone who has a sad personality by disposition has a problem, and cannot be happy in any aspect without a drug or narcotic.

A good attitude can have a positive influence on your life because it can set the terms for properly handling life's events, and, in particular, life events that involve working with or dealing with other people. What makes an attitude good is whether you approach life's issues as if expecting a positive outlook. A positive outlook signals to others you are in touch with positive feelings and disposed to positively handling the challenges of life and work.

I have read that many distressed people are consumed with worry about unhappy endings. The advice they are often given is: "To stop worrying, learn that you're in charge of your own head. You can choose to make up stories with happy instead of sad endings."[2]

The implication here is that you must *"make up"* happy endings to help you stop worrying. Why not just work to bring about happy endings by understanding your values and accomplishing them? The result (in reality) would be happy endings. Attitude and action are the keys to such happy endings.

The goal of this chapter is to develop a basis for a change of personal attitude, sometimes called a Sense of Life. Here, I will offer attitude-changing techniques to help people who have experienced discomfort over their inability to have a positive outlook.

The premise of this chapter is the simple idea that good things come to those with good attitudes. The basis for this notion is my own

---

[2] BOTTOM LINE PERSONAL.

personal experience. Having gone through the devastation that divorce and financial loss can exert on a person's emotions, I have had personal experience with both positive and negative attitudes and their impact on my ability to function properly. I will state, as an aside, that attitude is a characteristic that should be asserted, and, properly, the assertion of a positive egoism is a key to personal happiness. There should be no guilt felt by any human being seeking to assert his value in life and in the world.

Many people beset with a poor attitude have gotten this way because they think only the worst is possible to them. In fact, a bad attitude exacerbates negative thinking and blocks success. In fact, most people fight against that attitude throughout their lives, never realizing that within them, unstated, is the idea, that in the end, each individual is destined to fail.

If one always expects that something bad will

happen, then one will dismiss any good that can come. One will miss the opportunity to bring good into being. This deeper sadness has been identified as metaphysical malevolence geared against life and the individual. It is the enemy of attitude and happiness.

The feeling that bad things will happen is a myth that you would do well to discard. But that is not always an easy thing to do. Negative thinking can affect your general attitude for years until it is eradicated. In fact, the man-made world is sometimes a terrible place that complicates life. Fear, pain, suffering, dread, worry, and anxiety are common emotional consequences of the myth that bad things will always happen.

How can a person determine if his attitude needs a change? A man should always know how he feels. His inner thoughts will expose his inner mind and his subconscious evaluation of reality. If he feels anger, hate, spite, or fear, his attitude will likely be his nemesis, his enemy. These emotions are a key to your understanding of yourself and they should spur you to action to straighten out your intellectual house – your mind.

You need, first, to engage in introspection about your day-to-day thought processes. You should take daily inventory of your emotional life and determine just how much worrying you do. You need to ask yourself, "Do I often expect bad things to happen, or do I have an expectation for good outcomes?"

A diary of your attitudinal thoughts from day to day should be kept and regularly updated. If you notice an abundance of thoughts that the worst will probably happen, explore how it affects your mood, personality, and your basic approach to life and others. You will see progress over time that will help you change the attitude.

Poor attitude can create the failures of life. A person with a poor attitude is fighting a battle that can only lead to frustration and failure because it influences every aspect of his life. All negative attitudes reduce to the premise that something bad is going to happen. Yet, it is circular reasoning that causes this, a sort of self-fulfilling prophesy.

This circular reasoning about attitude is the modus operandi of the dis-enfranchised individual. Life is only as hard as you make it, so they say. It flies in the face of the notion that man is naturally adequate for survival, and it is only his mind that can cloud his true nature.

The person who holds that the purpose of his life is success, pleasure, and enjoyment, who knows that his foremost goal is self-fulfillment and self-satisfaction, will find that the achievement of happiness is easier with the right attitude. Practice a positive attitude because nothing improves without practice and practice can help you get over those moments when you might not be feeling so positive.

How to Manage your Attitude.

The best way to cultivate a good attitude is to think positively especially in circumstantial cases, on the fly, so to speak. When I wrote my book on Purpose,[3] I discovered an excellent exercise to help you cultivate a positive attitude. Essentially, it involved juxtaposing positive attitudes against their opposite negative attitudes and then considering the practical consequences.

This process enables you to solidify (in your mind) the kind of thinking you need in order to change negative attitudes into positive ones. Below is a table to use for positive and negative attitudes.

Life	Death
General Disposition	
Positive	Negative

---

[3] The Real Purpose-Driven Life https://amzn.to/3t6Tqwf (Paid link)

The basic positive attitude requires a focus on reality. The primacy of existence is the conviction that existence is primary and that understanding the nature of existence, the real, is paramount in having a positive attitude.	The negative is a focus on the zero, un-being, nothingness – there is no argument for it.
Light	Darkness
A metaphor that connotes positivity	A metaphor that connotes negativity
Peace of Mind – no worry about the future	Panic – always worry about what will happen
Peace of mind comes from certainty about reality. Existence Exists.	The future is uncertain because the mind is uncertain. The Supernatural can lead to doubt and fear.

Love of Mankind	Anger and Conflict with other men
This is a general view of man's nature. If you think man is generally good by nature you are prone to have better relations with people.	If you think men are evil by nature or weak, you will find lots of conflict with others and even yourself. Confusion is the result and so is failure.
Hope for good	Dread/Despair about the future
Hope is positive, an expectation that good will happen if one thinks and acts out of positive notions	This is anti-hope, the opposite of positive expectations. It is a very powerful force that suppresses happiness
Optimism	Pessimism
Optimism is another term for hope but more certain of a good outcome	Another term for despair but more philosophical as it is supported by a general sense of unreality

Metaphysics	
Existence	Non-existence/Nihilism (Primacy of Consciousness)
How to tie the positive to existence: Understand that existence is "the real" and you can only be positive about what you know with certainty. Certainty is knowing reality/existence. Existence has primacy in the mind – but more than this, it *is*.	Non-existence has no relation to existence/reality. It is a negative concept, and, in reality, the negative does not exist. Non-existence "is" "non", it has no presence in reality
Science	Mysticism

Science is the study of existence. It is based on the primacy of existence. Existence is the only reality and in logic that means A is A.	Mysticism is the contemplation and adherence to non-existence. It is the essence of negativity and is based on the false premise that consciousness, by itself, is the only reality. It is the practice of non-existence, the negative.
Truthful ideas and concepts	Falsehoods (False Characteristics create False Concepts
Truth can only be found by connecting concepts to existence. This is done by the individual defining his concepts according to "defining characteristics"	Falsehood comes from bad concepts that lead to lies or mistakenly defined characteristics. It can lead to false notions and eventually nihilism.
Knowledge	Ignorance

Knowledge results from good thoughts, good/true concepts which leads to true identification of reality and correct action based on reality.	Ignorance is the opposite of knowledge. It is based on bad thoughts, concepts wrongly defined which lead, in action to poor decisions.
Logical	Illogical
Takes the principle that "A is A" and applies it consistently to all thinking.	Rejects the principle that "A is A" and seeks a non-standard that leads to anti-mind and anti-man thinking.
Truth	The Irrational and Untrue
Truth = objectivity	Untruth is rejection of existence, the non-standard, the non-real, the non-man, the zombie.
Reason	Irrationality

Logic and objectivity applied to all thinking from A is A to the widest abstractions.	Thinks that logic is just a different opinion.
Reality	Supernatural
A synonym for "Existence", reality refers more specifically to the world of things and anything which is said to exist.	A world presumed by mystics to exist outside of the natural world. It describes the essence of mysticism and religion, a false concept that has not been "proven" to exist.
Morality	
Concerned about Positive Values and Achieving them	Concerned about what people think or do

Positive values are based on the standard of life. They lead to life and are based upon love of existence which is the source of all life and happiness.	Negative values are focused on the secondary views of others and therefore are disconnected from existence. They are haphazard and eventually destructive.
Active Living	Depression and Doubt
This is the development and active pursuit of values by means of integrating action around the goal of value pursuit.	This is the avoidance of active living by negative thinking.
Personal Situation	
Freedom of Action	Tension

Only a rational person, one connected to reality, can be free to act rationally.	The negative person is not free to act rationally. He has no order or consistency in his life because he is not connected to reality. His actions are controlled because that is the only action he can take.
In Charge of Your Life	Life is Controlled by Others
Requires life-serving decisions and actions. Requires reason.	Requires altruism and collectivism, dependence, and inability to make life-serving decisions.
Liberty	Fight/Flight/Freeze

Liberty refers to your freedom to make your own decisions in life and to live for your own self-interest.	The restriction of liberty (within the individual) is the response to fear of the opinions of others as they relate to your personal choices. Altruism is the source of these opinions of others.
Grounded	Uprooted
Grounded. Conceptual with well-defined concepts.	Separated from reality. The anti-conceptual mentality.
Happiness	Depression
The successful state of life when the mind is connected to reality and integrated with the body and its needs.	The failed condition when the mind is disconnected from reality by negative and faulty thinking methods and rationalizations.
Solid Personhood	Vulnerable

Habitual reliance on reason builds a solid person. Reason is the source of the human power to affect reality and survive well.	Vulnerable to the vicissitudes of reality-cause and effect-because weak or disconnected from reality. Vulnerable to evil men because one does not know they must be fought.
Independence of Mind and Ideas	Dependence of Mind and Ideas
Reason can only come from an independent mind.	The mind mired to dependence upon the ideas of other people will always be dependent.
Living	Dying
This is the ultimate choice that guides all thinking and acting.	The opposite (negative) of living.
Thinking	Brooding

True thinking is focusing on reality which yields tangible positive results and confidence.	Brooding is negative thinking about something wrong and negative emotions of anger and futility.
Consciousness	Unthinking and Unconsciousness
Consciousness of reality means a positive view of "what is". It is a process for knowing not for *making* reality.	Unthinking is relinquishing the responsibility. Unconsciousness is the absence of focus and unthinking about the real.
Mindfulness	Refusal to Think
The ability to use your mind in a self-directed way that will positively affect your life.	The conscious choice to let emotions guide your choices, sometimes automatized and automatic after a time.
Mind/Body Unity	Mind/Body Split

When mind and body are a unit, there is no conflict and the individual functions more efficiently and can achieve happiness.	When mind and body are split, there is conflict, disorder, and unhappiness.
Winning at Life	Losing at Life
Good values, good actions = love of life = happiness.	Disvalues, wrong actions = hatred of life = unhappiness.
Objective Thinking	Subjective Thinking
Objective reality – Primacy of Existence.	Primacy of Consciousness – Duty.
Full Relaxation	Unease and High Blood Pressure
Stress-free living – moral living, primacy of existence, peace of mind, integrated mind, and body.	Immoral living, primacy of consciousness, out of context thinking, concrete-bound thinking, anti-conceptual mentality, disease, mental disorder.

Healthy Eating	Unhealthy Eating
Count calories, sugar, cholesterol, sodium, etc. And eat right.	Eat to die, eat to make you feel better, to avoid life.
Happiness/Moral Living	Immoral Living
Defining values and making rational choices = happiness.	Having no standards of value. Making decisions emotionally = unhappiness. Refusal to think = misery.
Creating	Destroying or Not Creating
Creating requires knowledge of reality, imagination, and value-definition.	These require nothing and lead to depression and unhappiness. They lead eventually to "acting out" and nihilism.
Exercise/Activity	Sedentary/Inactivity

Keep energy flowing. Keep life flowing. Keep body active and efficacious.	Give life away. Cease activity. Give up. Die.
Organization of Life	Disorganization and Unconcern about Life
Focus on values and goals with life as the standard. Keep a written record of your values and order them hierarchically.	Floating through life. Give little thought to values. Ignore goals and plans. Live a disorganized life lacking hierarchy of values.
Know that the metaphysical world is not conscious	Believe that physical reality is a thinking entity
Objectivism – Accept the real and that it operates according to its nature and has no thought of choice	Mysticism – Reality is conscious – the world's worst and most dangerous concept. Reality does not think or act or choose

Judge the man-made	Fear men and what they do
This is an issue of justice and identifying whether the acts of people are positive or negative.	Fear of the thoughts of men and the refusal to judge represents and inordinate amount of fear of human consciousness. It implies the Primacy of Consciousness.
Competence (in myself)	Incompetence (in myself)
An active mind, practiced in reason, will achieve competence and precise thinking.	An inactive mind is an insecure mind.
Doing the right thing	Doing the wrong thing

The right thing is the moral thing. It requires looking at reality and thinking, the result is happiness and satisfaction.	Refusal to think leads to doing the wrong thing and leads to failure and unhappiness.
Admiration of competence in others	Disapproval of Inefficacy
This is a matter of justice – knowing of what is good and rewarding it.	Results from not thinking clearly or refusing to think. Admiring inefficacy is nihilism.
Reward value	Reward disvalue
Justice for the good is more important than punishing the evil.	Rewarding disvalue is the opposite of justice and harms the good.
Rational	Irrational

The rational mind is consistent in its adherence to reality. To be rational is to be correct.	The irrational avoids reason and is therefore wrong and failed. To be irrational is to be wrong.
Conceptual Definition accuracy	Conceptual Land Mine (poorly defined characteristics of concepts)
Clear, precise definitions mean clear, precise thinking. Not all concepts are created equal. Is there an issue you are dealing with that conceptual clarity can help you with?	Conceptual moral equivalency is a mixture of vague concepts with clear concepts – sloppy thinking. Moral travesty is thereby enabled. I call this the mixed economy of human thought.
Cognitive Precision	Cognitive Imprecision

Concepts are units of consciousness of reality. They are how you see. Their precision determines the accuracy of learning of reality.	Poorly defined concepts are the cause of failure and misunderstanding.
Integration of Knowledge	Disintegration of Knowledge
Since reality is an integrated whole, knowledge must be integrated with other knowledge. This yields full understanding.	Disintegration is the splitting or separation of knowledge. Miss-integration is "knowledge" based on mysticism and/or rationalism. They destroy man's focus (or scatter it) on reality and his acquisition of consistent knowledge.
Truth	Contradiction
Truth is the expression of what is real and actual.	Contradiction is the expression of what is not real or actual.

Personal Hygiene	
Shaved	Unshaved
Well-groomed	Scruffy/Dusty
Bathed	Unbathed
Teeth Brushed	Teeth Un-brushed
Physical Health	
Exercise Daily with Weights	Skip Exercise with Weights
Walk Daily	Skip Walk
Yoga Daily	Skip Yoga
Meditation Daily	Skip Meditation
Smiling/Laughing	Frowning/Crying
Healthy-range Blood Pressure Under 120/80	High Blood Pressure (Above 140 Systolic)
Relations with Others	
Trust	Prejudiced

| Recognition that there is Nothing to Fear from People – Love of People – Expressing Love or Appreciation to People – Thinking Positively about People | Fear of People/Need to Escape – Thinking that I Don't have the Energy for it – Wanting to Get Away from Them |

An important aspect of attitude is your decision to take on a role of leadership. A good leader "jumps in" and acts when action is called for. When others look around to see who is going to act, the leader will take it upon himself to act and guide others to a successful solution. He isn't afraid of what people think, he doesn't hold back. In fact, he is looking for precisely this situation in order to express his value and seize the opportunity to deliver value. And when the union boss criticizes him for doing something he is not paid to do, he ignores the charge and keeps giving value.

On the other hand, the leader is not a solitary loner. If he finds other individuals with good attitudes and leadership skills, he would rather be around such people. He makes friends across the organization and seeks to create a "culture of excellence", helping those like him and generating positive and value-sharing relationships. He also knows that the best way to be a good employee is to think like a manager, to understand the logic behind good business practices, and why it is important to always be a professional team player.

I once knew an employee of a major international corporation who came to work every day and waited for something to happen. He performed his routine activities, and when his work was done, he asked the boss if he could go home. When the company cut back, he was the first to go. On the other hand, his associate, doing the same work, always asked for more work when he was done. He was complimented during his performance review as part of the future of the company. Later, he was awarded a supervisory role and a percentage of the profits. I was proud to have recognized his ability and promoted him to management.

Another aspect of his good attitude was his willingness to listen to feedback and use it to improve his performance. His willingness to learn and his good results were more important to him than defending himself against criticism.

The Hines Story

In 1968, I was hired by UPS as a clerk. During my training, I was presented with a mimeographed sheet of paper and asked to read it. This text was given to every new UPS employee. It was common to hear: "Remember the Hines Story". No one ever told me the source of the story or the name of the writer. I repeat it here:

"Mr. Hines, the owner of the Hines Lumber Company recently had to fill a top executive position. Two of his managers with equal experience were considered but the choice went to the man who had fewer years with the company. Upon learning of the promotion, the other man asked Mr. Hines why he wasn't the one selected. Instead of answering him Mr. Hines asked him if any lumber had come in that day. The man said he would check and a few minutes later reported that a carload had arrived that morning. Mr. Hines then wanted to know the type of lumber. After again checking, the manager told him it was number 6 pine. Mr. Hines then asked the man how many board feet were in the order. Again, leaving the room to check he returned shortly with the answer of 3500 board feet. This type of questioning went on for several minutes and then Mr. Hines asked the man to sit in the next room, leaving the door ajar so he could still hear.

"Mr. Hines then called to the manager who had been promoted and asked him if any lumber had arrived that day. The manager said he would check, and, in a few minutes, he returned with the following answer. A carload of number 6 pine had come in on track three at 9:30 A.M. and totaled 3500 board feet. The lumber was unloaded by 2:00 P.M. and stored in warehouse number 18. It was order number 65-03 for the Williams Company and its total value was $16,352.00.

"Mr. Hines thanked the man and said he could go. After the second man left Mr. Hines called in the first manager who had heard the entire conversation. The first manager said he knows now why the other man had been promoted instead of himself."

Which employee are you; the one promoted or the one not promoted?

Let me make a few additional observations.

1. If you have "dead time" during your work day, what should you do? Answer: Ask your boss what you can do to help the company bring in more business. At the very least, ask him/her what you can do to improve your productivity or take on new responsibilities.
2. The individual who acts when called upon by management will be judged by the quality of that action. As we saw in the Hines Story, the successful individual was more thorough, and he gave the manager more than he ostensibly needed. In fact, that information was useful to the manager and saved him the time he would have spent waiting for the employee to come back with the answer to a new question. More is better when it comes to giving your boss value in return for your paycheck.

Most people who have dead time during their day, decide to hide from the boss. They see that dead time as a gift – they are getting paid for doing nothing. But is it a gift or a harbinger of disaster? If you are being paid for doing nothing, how can the company make a profit? If you hide and hope that your boss does not discover your dead time, you will be less valuable to the company simply because you said nothing and continued drawing a pay check. When it comes time to cut out the dead weight, who do you think will keep his job? You or the other employee who offered to work during his dead time?

If you have dead time at work, this means the profits of the company are being wasted. This situation must be fixed before the company goes out of business. So, you should make sure you are the solution (and not the problem), or you will be the one "out of business".

3. Don't argue with the boss – You are not smarter than he is, nor are you more valuable to the company than he is. Arguing with the boss makes you an adversary and that means you are a problem for the company. When the time comes to cut expenses, you'll be the one getting cut.

   This does not mean that you cannot offer your ideas on how to improve things; you should offer your views with good intentions and a desire to be of value to the company. But make sure the boss knows you are not complaining; convince him that you have a positive attitude before you criticize something that you think is wrong. Even if your boss is closed to your suggestions, he will at least see you as an employee seeking to be of value.

4. What if your boss is a poor manager and you don't like his leadership style? Answer: Don't assume that you know more than your boss. Don't confuse

personality conflicts with an inability of your boss to lead and direct you. Don't criticize the boss.

Management by Walking Around

I remember the barracks inspections during my army days. Our staff sergeants did not prepare us for what we later learned was "the white glove" inspection. On this day, the company commander walked in wearing white gloves to discover areas of the barracks where dust was spotted.

As he walked around the area looking for dust, we learned that if we had forgotten to clean certain areas, we would be "punished" by a long period of extra cleaning that took us away from our "free time" and left us languishing in the task of cleaning up.

As a UPS manager, we learned of the concept known as "Management by Walking Around" during which upper management engaged in the simple task of walking around the operational areas, offices, hub/package processing areas, etc. to simply observe. Later, the supervisors would learn what needed to be corrected in a special meeting held by the upper manager.

Management by Walking Around is a well-known tactic and was often used to communicate needed corrections by management. I recall, in particular, a scene that I observed during a trip to the garage area of the Indianapolis Motor Speedway. I observed Indy Car driver, Helio Castroneves, at that time, a three-time winner of the Indianapolis 500, as he grabbed a towel and cleaned the counters of the garage area. I imagined that he was thinking of being reprimanded by his boss Roger Penske had "threatened" a "white glove" inspection of the facility.

"What is managing by walking around? It is often called management by wandering around or MBWA for short, and was popularised by Tom Peters and Robert Waterman in their 1981 Book, "In Search For Excellence." Through their research of successful companies, they found that managers that walked around and engaged with their employees were far more effective than those that managed from their office. They labelled this MBWA. It's now one of a suite of management tools that allows management and their subordinates to discuss what's working, what's not, and what can be improved at the front line and where the work gets done. Doing this regularly, allows the team to share ideas, develop good practice and eradicate sub-standard behaviours and processes, as well as improve communication, trust, and rapport."[4]

After every new marketing initiative, we used MBWA by creating direct reports from managers and supervisors about "What went right", What went wrong" and "How it can be fixed.

---

[4] https://www.the10minuteleader.com/managing-by-walking-around/#:~:text=%203%20Components%20to%20The%20Management%20by%20Walking,the%20management%20norm%2C%20you%E2%80%99ll%20build%20a...%20More%20

Management by Objectives

"Management by Objectives (MBO) is a strategic approach to enhance the performance of an organization. It is a process where the goals of the organization are defined and conveyed by the management to the members of the organization with the intention to achieve each objective."[5]

At UPS, each individual was given monthly objectives which were quantified goals that the individual was supposed to accomplish. At the end of the month, he plotted numerically how he had accomplished his objectives. There are plenty of resources on the Internet that describe MBO processes that you can use to monitor corporate success from the individual on up to the departmental level.

---

[5] https://corporatefinanceinstitute.com/resources/knowledge/strategy/management-by-objectives-mbo/

Do not be a Marxist

Many of us have been indoctrinated by teachers or parents with an anti-capitalist bias. The father of anti-capitalism is Karl Marx who wrote the seminal works about communism which he held to be the next (inevitable) phase of historical development.

Communism has caused nothing but problems for the world. It has fomented wars and revolutions and introduced force and violence into human relationships. Marxists want to control rather than leave people free. Their claim that capitalism is evil is proven wrong by the fact that life for almost all people is improved by capitalism. Their premise that men should sacrifice for others is the flaw that proves them wrong. It is precisely because capitalism does not demand sacrifice that makes it good and productive.

If you believe in Marxism, there is no way you can be a good employee for a profit-seeking company. Don't blame it on the company; blame it on yourself. You need an attitude adjustment. If you think your boss is an exploiter you must seek to "expose" the company for the evil it does. You must think that your boss is a thief who needs to be punished for his activities. What would make you want to be productive for any company? Kiss your chances of employment good bye.

In fact, Marxists are wrong about capitalism. Capitalism is not a "system" in the sense that it gives people the power to exploit others. Capitalism merely enables freedom, voluntary cooperation, consensual trade, and voluntary labor agreements. Capitalism exploits no one because it has no mechanism for the use of force against individuals. Capitalism is the absence of force in human relationships, and this makes it good.

You can go on to study Marxism if you want. You will find that Marxism is based upon historical materialism, the idea that history moves according to a class struggle that developed centuries before capitalism came along. It flies in the face of the fact that capitalism destroyed the class system in every sense. In addition, capitalism enables an individual, born into poor circumstances, to rise to the level of a millionaire and enjoy abundance through hard work and ingenuity.

This last fact is totally ignored by Marxists who have fallen for a false critique of capitalism. Marx saw political power and coercion in everything that capitalism brought to the world. But Marx's critique of capitalism was based upon false arguments. Capitalism brought no coercion to society. It meant freedom; contracts were not force or slavery but mutual agreements where both parties agreed to engage in win/win situations. So, when capitalism kept improving people's lives, Marxists kept seeing the next tipping point in its destruction. The result is that Marxist manipulation (force), designed to interfere and "fix" capitalism, only served to force and enslave individuals under coercive and dictatorial governments.

Marx posited a historical struggle based upon economic movements which, in fact, cannot happen. Reality does not implement "ideas"; it can only move according to cause and effect as it relates to entities. This means that entities (even human beings) act according to their natures. There is no such thing as a universal or "metaphysical" economic class. There is only reality, and it is the purpose of man's consciousness to identify and understand reality by identifying entities, abstractions, and principles. All abstractions are derived from man's conceptual awareness; they are not universal movements, essences, or entities.

You may not think this is an important issue, but I'd like to remind you that Marx posited that his economic determinism was a universal principle. Yet, absolute reality cannot implement economic classes; only a conceptual mentality can do this by understanding principles of reality. Concepts do not exist in a vacuum but within the context of other human knowledge. This means that Marx is wrong about his metaphysical and epistemological principles. Class is not determinative of anything metaphysical. You determine your "status" through your thinking and hard work.

John Paul Getty – the Three Rules to Riches

One of J. Paul Getty's famous quotes is "Formula for success: rise early, work late, strike oil". These words are among the most repeated from the venerable billionaire who became rich in the oil industry. It is a simple, but very true, formula for success. If you follow it, you will not fail. Here's why:

"Rise Early"

Getting up early to go to work gives you a tremendous advantage. While you are thinking, acting, working, and producing early in the morning, everyone else is sleeping or drinking their morning coffee. I've often noticed, in my own work, that working while others are celebrating, such as weekends or holidays, gave me a tremendous competitive advantage (in spite of the fact that I also had to raise my own daughter). I had used some of my time off to gain new knowledge while they were relaxing and enjoying their time off. I used some of my time to do something or invent something while they were grilling on the Barbee. I used some of my time to plan what I would do during the next work day while they used their time watching weekend television shows, going to the movies, dancing, drinking, and laughing. I did not envy them because later they would envy me for my success. I was building my skills while their skills were eroding away.

"Work Late"

Other versions of this quote use the term "work hard" instead of "work late".

I think working hard is all about production as is the term working late, since working late enables more production. In fact, every product on the planet that is offered for sale is based upon a human scale. This means that it is for the benefit of humans and/or of such a size that humans make them and use them. Working hard or working late mean working with all of one's strength and energy to accomplish a specific task that will benefit customers. Working hard/late means doing one's best and delivering top quality results.

Another aspect of "working hard" is that some types of work are difficult to accomplish because they require human strength and physical ability to accomplish. Think of the mechanic who must work on heavy parts and engines through his muscle power. He must know how machines operate and what makes them work, as well as how to fix them, but he must also have the physical strength to do the job. Not every individual is able to do this work and those who are able to do it have more value and deserve good salaries. Turning a wrench is certainly working hard and it accomplishes value for the operator of the machine being fixed.

"Strike oil"

This term is a metaphor for producing a product that most people need. This condition of offering needed products implies that many people will buy the product and that means higher profits and riches for the producer. You do not necessarily have to produce oil or oil products; this term refers to anything you can make that is wanted by many people. The more people who want your product, the richer you become. Strategic planning is the work of projecting the number of potential customers and then developing the products and methods that will deliver them to people.

Discovering Concepts and How to Use them in Business

In this chapter, I'm going to provide you with an approach to thinking that will make you a better employee and maximize your professional success. I call it the conceptual approach.

A concept is a mental unit of thought that refers to an idea, principle, or thing in the real world. A concept is defined through a verbal description that identifies the defining characteristics of the things or facts to which it refers. Defining characteristics are those that make the referent what it is, that make it different from all other things.

The concept is the tool that humans use when trying to understand and act in the real world. It is expressed both verbally and in written form as a word that implies all of its relevant characteristics.

You cannot advance beyond the level of a primitive human being without the competent use of concepts. Not only do concepts exist for virtually every "thing" you deal with, but they also enable you to think "abstractly" with higher level knowledge such as theories, principles, and the widest abstractions that are not directly connected to the perceptual level of consciousness. In fact, the singular reason that people do not advance in life beyond lower-level jobs is because they are not efficient users of more advanced concepts; they are mired in perceptual concretes and are unable to think the kinds of thoughts that would make them more valuable than those who can only do manual labor.

Creating a new concept is not about creating a new word. It is about defining a new thing or relationship and learning how to use it mentally. If a new concept is valid (properly defined and used), it represents an open door to new knowledge, new actions, and a new understanding that benefits life. If a new concept is invalid (which means it is not adequately connected to reality) it leads to ignorance and closes the door to new knowledge and successful action.

For instance, let's assume you discover a new

fact of reality. Let's say you have discovered a new extract from a plant that makes people with insomnia sleep better. To retain the fact of the existence of this extract in memory you need to create a concept. The defining characteristic about this drug is that it contains a new chemical ingredient that you are going to call "Icosleep". You name the drug after yourself, let's say "Roberts". "Roberts" contains the characteristic which is the extract you have identified as Roberts "Icosleep" which, when ingested by insomniacs, helps them sleep.

You now have a new concept, a new drug, a new benefit and once put into production for sale, a new product. Later, you might find other uses for this product such as anesthesia benefits and possibly the fact that it helps pregnant women handle labor. Each of these represents new benefits and additional medical improvements none of which were possible without your discovery of icosleep.

This process of thinking is called concept formation and it has tremendous benefits for the business professional. Once a new concept is identified, it takes, in a sense, a life of its own. If it is a highly useful concept, it becomes culturally important and opens the possibility of derivative concepts which open the doors for even more concepts and uses. A good example is the concept of electricity which spawned many new inventions and other areas of knowledge. You could not have had the light bulb (and many other concepts) without the concept of electricity.

What is a definition and how can we discover valid definitions? A definition is a description of a specific concept. Definitions can refer to concrete existents as well as abstract relationships that represent principles of thought or action. The study of metaphysics deals with the nature of existence and the study of epistemology deals with how man gains knowledge. The answer to this last question is "through concepts".

How does one verify that a concept is real? One does it by conceptualizing the entity through a valid definition then looking at reality to see if it exists as it is defined. This can be done anecdotally or scientifically (through a specialized process tailored to its validation). Generally, the scientific process is engaged in by experts in the field who are capable of such studies.

Generally, one understands a concept by means of its defining characteristic/s and by investigating its place or function. For abstract concepts, concepts that identify a principle rather than a thing, one does it by going beyond perception into the relationships of previously defined concepts. One ties each concept to verifiable facts and relationships. This process is called reduction.

As a starting point, here are some important rules for understanding and using concepts:

1. Your understanding of reality and your thinking methods must be correct if you want to effectively use concepts to make ethical business decisions. You must clearly define your concepts in order to decide what to do.

    a. This implies that you can direct your

conscious processes, focus, and consciously analyze and use concepts, analyze stored knowledge, ask questions, find answers, and devise the foundation upon which you will make decisions and take proper action.

2. Your ethical reasoning process must be based on facts, and be contextually and logically correct. By having correct referents, you can successfully connect to reality and deal with all obstacles to accomplish long-term goals.

 a. This implies that long-term goals are the proper basis upon which to identify specific acts during every-day decision-making.

 b. This implies that life should be the standard of concept formation and correct decisions.

 c. Concepts are the tools of reason, and you must follow the principles of correct knowledge development.

3. Free will influences all thinking processes. You have the freedom to choose to question every thought, conclusion or thought process.

Concepts are the building blocks to knowledge and appropriate action. Correctly defined concepts provide content to your thoughts, and they spur more and better thinking. To learn more about concepts and how to use them, see the book *Introduction to Objectivist Epistemology* by Ayn Rand.

Free Will

Free Will is essentially the choice to think or not to think. This decision leads to human action or lack thereof. How can it help you as an employee in the business world?

Harry Binswanger, in his booklet, "Volition as Cognitive Self-Regulation", writes "Man is the rational animal. He has the ability to form abstractions, i.e., concepts. That vastly expand the range of his awareness.

"Man's rational faculty includes not only the ability to conceptualize the world in which he must act, but also the ability to conceptualize his mental processes as such. This gives man an entirely new level of self-regulation: the ability to regulate, with limits, the actions of his consciousness, which in turn regulate his existential actions. It is this capacity for regulating the operations of his own mind that underlies much of what makes him distinctively human: the ability to act long-range against the pull of immediate pleasures and pains, to correct his thinking by means of logic, to correct even automatized, subconscious misevaluations (as in overcoming neurosis), and to forge his own character in the image of his self-idea."

Free will (or volition) is the first step in the process of self-regulation of your mental processes. This choice (to think or not to think) represents the fundamental choice for you. If you choose to think, then you open the door to using all the mental and intellectual tools you need to be successful (We will cover many of these below). On the other hand, if you choose not to think regarding your career, then the door closes and none of the possibilities that attend thinking are possible.

Free Will can mean a great deal to your success. Let's look at some of the ways it can help you succeed:

How to Think

When you choose to think, to focus, you have taken a very important step in developing your career. But it is only the beginning. There is a great deal more to it and thinking is not for the lazy person. You start by learning how to think and for that you need logic.

All thinking is conceptual. The concept is the basic unit of thought. Thinking ranges from **no concept/no thought** to the **concept** then to the **proposition** which is a statement (a syllogism) of the relationship between two concepts each having known knowledge. It is at the stage of the proposition that thinking takes off and knowledge begins to grow.

A concept is identified by a definition. A definition is the statement of the distinguishing characteristics of an entity or concept as it exists. A proposition is the statement of a fact that comprises a unit of knowledge. It is structured according to the principle "A is A". For instance, the statement "I am hungry" is a proposition that identifies a physical state that requires nutrition. A proposition is made up of a subject and a predicate separated by a relationship between the two. "I" is the subject of the proposition and "hungry" is the predicate (that which is being said about the subject) and "am" is the expression of the relationship between subject and predicate.

The syllogism is the expression of the relationship between two statements. There are rules for correctly using the syllogism that can help you determine truth. The identification of those rules is illustrated by a diagram that can help in understanding how to handle a syllogism (the graph is in the chapter named "Logic").

The Importance of Focus

After you have chosen to think, the next part of the process is focus. Focus is also a volitional process. It involves exerting mental energy to give attention to the facts that will influence your decisions.

What is focus? How do you do it? How can it help you? Focus is the exertion of mental energy toward a specific mental action that takes in information (or facts) that need to be known. It also processes information, integrating it into past knowledge and/or edifying past knowledge. You do it by isolating an entity or a principle and asking questions that will produce information and/or knowledge. Focus can make it possible for you to act in an informed way that accomplishes beneficial results and goals.

When is it time to focus? Whenever you have a need for knowledge that will help you achieve a specific goal or solve a particular problem. The tools of focus are the laws of logic which ensure that you are using time-tested universally accepted principles of thought that apply across time.

I don't have the space in this book to give you an entire course on how to think logically. There are several excellent online sources that can give you the training you need to begin the process. Believe it or not, I don't think you can get such a training in most universities; most professors are not equipped to give you a clear understanding of what logic is and how to think logically. You need to develop the ability to routinely think according to proven logical methods and I would suggest the next chapter as a good beginning.

Logic

Many people, even school teachers, don't know what logic is. In fact, most of the time, when I've tried to introduce logic to people, I am treated as if I am introducing a political opinion that should be doubted. Logical thinking is not about ideology or a set of political ideas. It is about correct thinking and that means thinking that is right and true. It has nothing to do with feelings or random opinions.

Yet, some people will even ask, whose thinking are you talking about, yours or mine? The implication is that there is no such thing as truth and that all ideas are merely opinions of individuals who should be doubted. This is called polylogism.

Polylogism is the idea that there are different systems of logic, and that one system is just as good as another. This is untrue. Logic is about method, finding the correct methods for understanding reality. The rules of logic are universal in the sense that they apply in all situations. They are not limited and varied;

they are simply true. For instance, the Law of Identity states that "A is A" which means that in all situations a thing is what it is. The Law of Excluded Middle states that a thing cannot be A and not A in any given context. It is either A or not A given the same context of human thought.

Here's a clue: anyone who says that logic does not work in gaining truth, is trying to keep you from gaining truth. Logic should be considered the "laws of thought".

The term "laws of thought" means a uniformity by which all people think and reason. Such laws are natural, and we do not have the power to change them. Every science pursues the natural laws of a specific area of study. Another definition: Logic is "the science of the necessary forms of thought." A form of thought is something that remains constant while it can be made to hold various types of content.

A form of reasoning is diagramed below. If M is S and S is P then M is P. This syllogism is true regardless of the make-up of M, S or P.

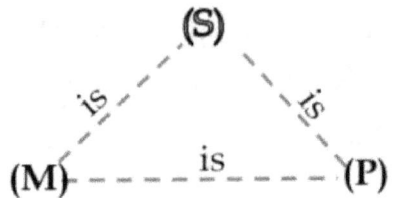

Logic, then, is the science that defines and describes the forms of thought so you can reason correctly according to reality. These forms are built upon simple and basic principles that apply across all possible content and subject matter.

All the sciences are required to operate according to logical forms because logical forms apply to all of reality and each science is charged with the task of dealing with a specific aspect of reality but according to logical forms. Logic keeps human thinking on track because it is the foundation of all knowledge.

Cause and Effect

Once we learn about the principle of Identity (A is A; a thing is what it is), we can learn to use the principle of causality, also known as the Law of Cause and Effect. The idea that every action produces a reaction is one simple way to say it; but it is much more than this. A thing acts (or reacts) according to its nature and knowing its nature can help you learn how it will act or react. This applies to both living and non-living entities.

The key to understanding causality is understanding concept formation, which requires that we identify the distinguishing characteristics of any concept that we are defining. A distinguishing characteristic is the characteristic (or group of characteristics) that make a thing what it is. By correctly identifying these characteristics within a relevant context, one can understand reality as well as project causal relationships.

Projecting causal relationships is a key ability for great managers. The accuracy of his or her thinking leads to better decisions especially those that involve many people and thousands of dollars. One can't be successful without having a clear understanding of the real world.

How do we move from the concept of causality to actually identifying how things will act in the real world? That's called "testing" or "the scientific method" which will most likely be different with each entity we are working with. The key is to put a theory or hypothesis to the test by setting up circumstances that will enable you to draw conclusions about how entities and/or ideas will actually work in the real world. Another name for "testing" is called induction and is a vast field of study that is responsible for most of man's knowledge and inventions.

Forms of the LOGICAL THINKING

If logic doesn't work, then it isn't logic that you are using. The study of logic is about studying the valid forms of thought which apply across all human thinking. If you use the correct form of thought according to the relevant rules of logic, then you should be able to ascertain true propositions about reality.

Logic is not just someone's opinion (although that has been argued); it is about the rules you need to follow if your thinking is to correspond to reality. Logic recognizes that reality is one and only one; there are not several realities; and, in order to understand reality, we need rules of thinking that work *in* that one reality.

There are two basic forms of logic: induction and deduction. More is known about deduction because Aristotle wrote extensively on the topic of how to derive truths by examining two statements (premises or propositions).

Most argumentation today is induction-based. People talk and think in terms of what they know from their own study, expertise, or experience. They use facts, statistics, deductions, and principles to understand reality and bring about their goals and plans (accomplish their values). When they argue, they answer the questions "what are the facts and how do I know it?".

So, when someone asks you what the weather is like today, you answer after you look around, feel the temperature on your body, look for and feel the rain on your skin (or by looking outside the window) and answer "warm and rainy". What you have just done is induction and deduction. After identifying the facts, you say, in essence, that "A is A"; you express the proposition: "It is rainy and warm". You can even go further toward a deduction:

It is rainy today.
When it rains, use an umbrella.
I will use an umbrella.

In other words,

All S is P
If P, then umbrella
Umbrella

Hundreds of millions of thought processes are engaged every day along similar lines. The key for each business person is to come up with usable knowledge and let that knowledge inform correct business decisions.

Induction

One of the most famous examples of induction was one of the first instances when an individual looked at reality and made a judgment. This individual had made for himself a new tool of observation called a telescope. At the time in which he lived, it was thought that the planets revolved around the earth and that the earth was the center of the universe. Galileo, on the other hand, used his telescope to scan the heavens and, after seeing the moons of Jupiter, decided that Copernicus (who had claimed that the sun was the center of the solar system) was correct and that the earth was not the center of the universe, that all the planets revolved around the sun. The Church insisted that the Bible clearly proved that the earth was the center of the universe and that questioning this "truth" was apostacy.

Galileo was harshly punished by the Church when he was sentenced to house arrest for the rest of his life. Yet, he clearly knew that he was correct. He knew that facts were necessary for correct knowledge, and, for you, facts are essential in your determination of correct business decisions.

As with Galileo, facts start with direct perception of reality and knowledge comes from evaluating those facts, determining their proper context and their specific meaning for the question being investigated. Whether you are investigating a topic for the sake of gaining knowledge or for the sake of improving production at work, the process should give you truth that you can use; truth that brings tangible results and benefits. Such is the nature of valid knowledge.

This means that the conclusions you draw must be usable and have real consequences. Therefore, effective leaders jump in, when confronted with the need for a decision. They engage in efforts to collect all the "facts" regarding important questions. This is leadership with knowledge and that's the best kind of leadership.

Induction is the process of discovering new knowledge through investigation while deduction starts with accepted premises. As we will see in the next section, induction seeks to discover facts and make true statements, premises, or propositions.

Let's assume you are trying to decide which cell phone will help you do your job. The conclusion you want to reach is "Cellphone X is my choice". The deductive syllogism would be:

- The selected phone should have the most business features.
- Cell phone X has the most business features I need.
- I should buy Cellphone X.

Having the most business features for a cell phone is not the only category of study. You may want to know the quality of those business features; but also, the range of the phone, how wide is the service area, how good is the sound, how difficult is it to carry. You may have a whole host of questions that help you decide on the right phone, and you may have to make several arguments for it depending upon what is important to your company. Each argument will have to investigate different facts and qualities so your solution will be the best possible for your ability to do business.

Induction is the process of developing new knowledge by testing reality and arriving at conclusions. This is sometimes called the scientific method because it is based on developing real knowledge by means of testing or experimentation. The tests are designed to investigate the facts as they relate to areas where there is little knowledge. The inductive process is designed to arrive at conclusions which can be validated and converted into new knowledge.

Deduction

The first basic form of the syllogism is called Barbara. Algebraically, it states the following:

All M are P.
All S are M.
All S are P.

As we saw earlier, one diagrammatic way of understanding Barbara is the following:

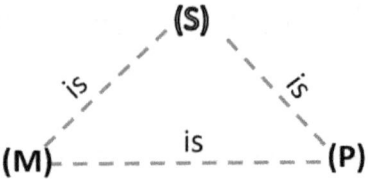

The overall structure of a syllogism is diagrammed as below:

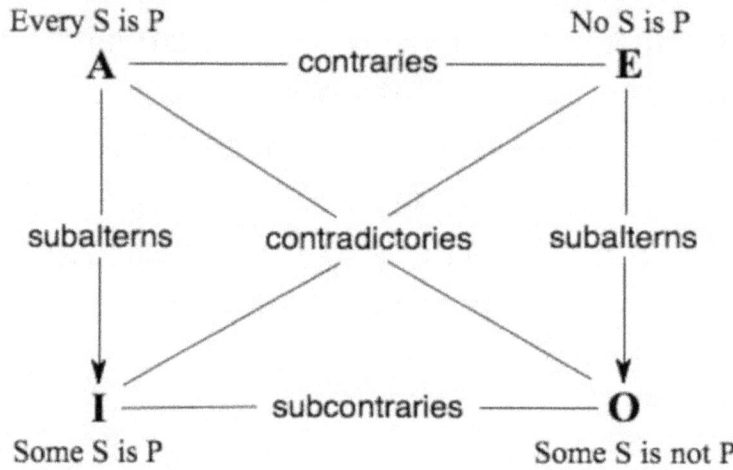

What we have above is the structure for categorical propositions. With such propositions, the important issue is not the content of the arguments but the forms; and there are only four such forms of argument.

A: Universal affirmative. All A are B
I: Particular affirmative. Some A are B
E: Universal negative. No A is B
O: Particular negative. Some A are not B

Each of these propositions are remembered by means of the letters A, I, E, and O:

"A" and "I" are from the Latin "Affirmo", "I affirm", while "E" and "O" are from the Latin "Nego", "I deny".

Categorical propositions are "universal affirmative" when they describe a relationship between the two terms (subject and predicate). This relationship is "distributed" in A and E because it discusses all units covered by the subject. The terms are "universal negative" in E and "particular affirmative" in I.

The letters you see in the diagram (A, E, I, O) are used to simplify the syllogism. There are fifteen types of syllogism, the first of which is known as **BARBARA**.

    A. All M are P.
    A. All S are M.
    A. All S are P.

Understanding logic and knowing how to be logical is a vast subject. I suggest taking an introductory course on logic at a local university or purchasing lecture courses on CD or digital formats and spending considerable time in understanding how to engage in both deduction and induction.

Logical Fallacies

Logic, properly used, creates truth and knowledge. As we have seen, it involves the rules of the syllogism and inductive reasoning. But the study of correct thinking is a wide subject, the knowledge of which could make you a better business person. It may take you some time to become proficient at strictly following the formal rules of logical deliberation and you should not feel bad about it.

Logicians, starting with Aristotle, have developed a few useful "short-cuts" to thinking logically called the informal fallacies. These fallacies often take their Latin names. Here are, apart from the first, their English names:

- Ad Hominem (Appeal to the man) "(Attacking the person): This fallacy occurs when, instead of addressing someone's argument or position, you irrelevantly attack the person or some aspect of the person who is making the argument. The fallacious attack can also

be direct to membership in a group or institution."[6]
- **Appeal to Ignorance**
"This fallacy occurs when you argue that your conclusion must be true, because there is no evidence against it. This fallacy wrongly shifts the burden of proof away from the one making the claim."[7]
- **Begging the Question (Petitio Principii)**
"...assuming what is to be proved in order to prove it."[8] Offering your conclusion as proof of your thesis.
- **Confusion of Necessary with a Sufficient Condition**

"A causal fallacy (is committed) when you assume that a necessary condition of an event is sufficient for the event to occur. A necessary condition is a condition that must be present for an event to occur. A sufficient condition is a condition or set of conditions that will produce the event. A necessary

---

[6] http://www.txstate.edu/philosophy/resources/fallacy-definitions/Ad-Hominem.htm l

[7] http://www.txstate.edu/philosophy/resources/fallacy-definitions/Appeal-to-Ignorance.html

[8] An Introduction to Logic by H. W. B. Joseph, Second Edition Revised, Oxford At the Clarendon Press, Page 590

condition must be there, but it alone does not provide sufficient cause for the occurrence of the event. Only the sufficient grounds can do this. In other words, all of the necessary elements must be there."[9] (Parentheses mine)

- Equivocation
  Equivocation is "…where a single word is used in divers senses."[10]
- False Dilemma
  "When you reason from an either-or position and you haven't considered all relevant possibilities, you commit the fallacy of false dilemma."[11]
- Faulty Analogy
  "This fallacy consists in assuming that because two things are alike in one or more respects, they are necessarily alike in some other respect."[12]

---

[9] http://www.txstate.edu/philosophy/resources/fallacy-definitions/Confusion-of-Necessary.html

[10] An Introduction to Logic by H. W. B. Joseph, Second Edition Revised, Oxford At the Clarendon Press, Page 579

[11] http://www.txstate.edu/philosophy/resources/fallacy-definitions/False-Dilemma.html

[12] http://www.txstate.edu/philosophy/resources/fallacy-definitions/Faulty-Analogy.html

- Inconsistency
  "A person commits the fallacy of inconsistency when he or she makes contradictory claims."[13]
- Irrelevant Authority
  "The fallacy of irrelevant authority is committed when you accept without proper support for his or her alleged authority, a person's claim, or proposition as true. Alleged authorities should only be used when the authority is reporting on his or her field of expertise, the authority is reporting on facts about which there is some agreement in his or her field, and you have reason to believe he or she can be trusted. Alleged authorities can be individuals or groups. The attempt to appeal to the majority or the masses is a form of irrelevant authority. The attempt to appeal to an elite or select group is a form of irrelevant authority."[14]

---

[13]http://www.txstate.edu/philosophy/resources/fallacy-definitions/Inconsistency.html

[14]http://www.txstate.edu/philosophy/resources/fallacy-definitions/Irrelevant-Authority.html

- Is Ought
  "The is-ought fallacy occurs when the assumption is made that because things are a certain way, they should be that way. It can also consist of the assumption that because something is not now occurring, this means it should not occur. In effect, this fallacy asserts that the status quo should be maintained simply for its own sake. It seeks to make a value of a fact or to derive a moral imperative from the description of a state of affairs."[15]
- Ought Is
  "The ought-is fallacy occurs when you assume that the way you want things to be is the way they are. This is also called wishful thinking. Wishful thinking is believing what you want to be true no matter the evidence or without evidence at all, or assuming something is not true, because you do not want it to be so."[16]
- Questionable Cause

---

[15] http://www.txstate.edu/philosophy/resources/fallacy-definitions/Is-ought.html

[16] http://www.txstate.edu/philosophy/resources/fallacy-definitions/Ought-Is.html

"This fallacy occurs when a causal connection is assumed without proof. All too often claims to a causal connection are based on a mere correlation. The occurrence of one event after the other or the occurrence of events simultaneously is not proof of a causal connection."[17]

- Red Herring
"This fallacy consists in diverting attention from the real issue by focusing instead on an issue having only a surface relevance to the first."[18]

- Slippery Slope
"In a slippery slope argument, a course of action is rejected because, with little or no evidence, one insists that it will lead to a chain reaction resulting in an undesirable end or ends. The slippery slope involves an acceptance of a succession of events without direct evidence that this course of events will happen."[19]

---

[17] http://www.txstate.edu/philosophy/resources/fallacy-definitions/Questionable-Cause.html

[18] http://www.txstate.edu/philosophy/resources/fallacy-definitions/Red-Herring.html

[19] http://www.txstate.edu/philosophy/resources/fallacy-definitions/Slippery-Slope.html

- Straw Person (Straw Man)
"This fallacy occurs when, in attempting to refute another person's argument, you address only a weak or distorted version of it. Straw person is the misrepresentation of an opponent's position or a competitor's product to tout one's own argument or product as superior. This fallacy occurs when the weakest version of an argument is attacked while stronger ones are ignored."[20]
- Two Wrongs
"If you try to justify an act/belief by pointing out in others a similar act/belief, you are committing the fallacy of "two wrongs make a right." This fallacy can occur by suggesting "if others are doing it, I can too" (common practice). Another form of the fallacy occurs when you dismiss a criticism of your action/belief, because your critic is acting/believing in

---

[20]http://www.txstate.edu/philosophy/resources/fallacy-definitions/Straw-Person.html

a similar way (you do it, too)."[21]
- **Unwarranted Generalization**
"This fallacy occurs when we make a generalization on the basis of insufficient evidence. This may occur when we rely on too small of a sample or an unrepresentative sample to support the generalization."[22]

There are literally hundreds of logical fallacies. You can find books full of them, but those listed above are the most common. It would do you well to learn them thoroughly and integrate them into your personal database of thinking. By learning to recognize when someone commits a logical fallacy, you will go a long way toward solving real problems. When you can recognize a logical fallacy in practice, you will have a clue to the kind of thinking others generally make and avoid the pitfalls of wrongful thinking.

---

[21] http://www.txstate.edu/philosophy/resources/fallacy-definitions/Two-Wrongs.html

[22] http://www.txstate.edu/philosophy/resources/fallacy-definitions/Unwarranted-Generalization.html

When a person uses an informal fallacy, he is betraying his own cognitive inefficacy, his inability to think clearly. Your knowledge of these fallacies can help you promote better ideas and solutions for the problems of running a business. This will help you stand out as a valuable employee.

Decision-Making

Every decision you make should be based upon the relevant facts of the situation that gives rise to the need for a decision. These facts can be broken down into positive statements (propositions and conclusions) that can be checked against reality (proven). You arrive at these conclusions and propositions by means of investigation (also called induction).

Effective decision-making can only take place when you use the best available knowledge. The jump from your knowledge to the correct decision is much easier if you apply the principles we discussed in our chapters on logic and logical fallacies.

Decision-making can only be based upon induction and analysis of the facts of reality as they relate to the field upon which you must decide. Essentially, there are three steps:

1. Identify the question about which the decision is to be made, and
2. Identify the facts that relate to that question, and
3. Draw your conclusion.

Decision-Making Worksheet

Decision-Making Worksheet
Date:
Individuals involved in this decision
Question
Relevant Facts
Needed Knowledge
How Will You Apply this Knowledge?

What tests or analyses will I need to make?
Results of test or analysis – list as bullet points
Decision (give reasons)

Who will implement the decision?
How will the decision be implemented?
When will the decision be implemented?
Who will be responsible for maintaining any necessary actions and to whom will they report?

Problem Solving

In this section, we refer to business problems that haunt the company. They can be such things as inefficient business processes, the use of faulty equipment in production, personnel policies, and standards of quality, etc. Such problems cause a business to lose money, perform disappointingly or harm company morale. When a business problem is solved, the company becomes stronger and improves its standing with customers.

As an employee, you add value to the company when you consider yourself part of the solution rather than part of the problem. Problem solving is a skill that all the best managers have. They don't hold back and they never settle for situations that keep the company from fulfilling its mission.

The first thing to do to solve a business problem is to describe the problem and the negative consequences of the problem. Quantify these consequences if possible. Then, use the process of induction to identify a solution that has a "possible" better consequence.

Implementing the solution is also very important. Someone should be charged with the responsibility for taking the actions that will solve the problem and a reporting process should be maintained. As this process moves forward, adjustments should be made as needed to improve the solution and focus it specifically on the problem.

It is always important to realize that it is the boss's or owner's responsibility to sanction your work and make the final decision to change procedures and fix the problem. Make sure you have his or her blessing for anything you do to solve the problem.

Problem Solving Worksheet

Problem Solving Worksheet
Date:
Individuals involved in this investigation
Problem
Statistics or Measurement Criteria
What is the Specific Cause of this Problem?

What is the Specific Business Process that is affected by this Problem?

Describe the Steps of this Business Process

What Specific Step is Responsible for this Problem?

What New Step/s Will Solve this Problem?

Describe the New Business Process with the New Steps

Perform some tests of this new procedure and measure the result. Then calculate the effect of the new procedure if all people performing this process were to do so.

Meet with and Report Results to the Director in Charge. Report the Results of the Meeting Here:

Next Step: (Do Another Worksheet or Implement the Procedure Company-Wide)

Pragmatism

This may seem like an overly philosophical issue, but I think it is important for business professionals not to get dragged into a way of thinking that is negative for their companies.

Top business professionals are often praised for their fact-based decision making. When working with a team, they want to be told "the facts"; they want it straight from the horse's mouth so they can make an informed decision. They don't like vague language, guesses or noncommittal responses. If you bring him or her a problem, they'd also like for you to bring a solution as well. They are problem solvers, no nonsense thinkers and, above all, they know how to get things done. This is called being pragmatic. But is it really? There is a difference between being pragmatic in the philosophical sense and being practical in the objective sense.

The first premise of pragmatic thinking is the belief that "perception is reality". The implication of such a view is that the human mind creates reality by merely thinking that something is true. This means that the mind creates facts which is not possible.

This view is based upon the philosophical notion that the human mind creates reality by thinking it. This notion, although accepted by most philosophy teachers in our universities, is untrue. Reality is independent of consciousness. It cannot be created by a wish of a god, an individual or a society full of individuals. If a fact is true, it is true because it is independently existent, not the product of the whims, emotions, or thoughts of people.

As we saw in our discussion of logic, a fact is an existent which is described by means of a proposition or statement. The statement "A is A" is a fact regardless of who disagrees. "The dog barks" is a fact. Neither of these facts can be created by the mind but must be acknowledged as facts. Therefore, it is not practical to think that perception is reality. Perception merely observes reality, and the mind can only acknowledge the existence of what is perceived.

The difference between the pragmatist view to practicality and the objective view is that the pragmatist focuses more on the opinions of others and the objectivist focuses on the facts.

It is the difference between accomplishment in reality and taking public opinion polls.

The next premise of pragmatism is that, in the realm of action, the only thing men can do is appeal to the opinions of others rather than ascertain independent facts. Because reality is unknowable, under this view, the only way to deal with reality is to take what are called "bold leaps". A bold leap is essentially a move to do something, anything to see how it works. When you hear that a business person is "results-oriented", to a pragmatist, it means that he takes bold leaps but monitors the results to see if it they are successful.

Why is this a problem? Most of the time, bold leaps are just a shot in the dark. There is very little in the way of "fact-gathering" involved. And this means, more than taking a bold leap; it means jumping off a cliff.

There is a better way and that is the way of induction as we saw in our chapter on Decision-Making. You can use facts and induction to decide what to do; you don't need to hope for the best; it is possible to know the best solution through careful study and knowledge acquisition.

Parenthetically, the pragmatic approach is why government programs work so poorly. Most politicians are pragmatists of the highest order. They were educated in our universities that practical action was pragmatic action. Pragmatism is not practical. The best approach is to look at reality, understand that the mind can rely on its perceptions and use concepts to solve problems.

Generating New Ideas

This chapter will show you how to generate new ideas. New ideas are the never-thought-of-ideas that bring change and innovation to business processes as well as the free market system. They are the hallmark of human progress and the basis upon which new companies and new products are based. Your ability to generate new ideas will be critical to your success in business.

New ideas are the innovations in your field. They represent, most often, the next step of product development for your already good products.

Each product that your company sells is made up of features and benefits. Each product, feature and benefit is a separate concept. The key to creating new ideas that improve your products and make up new products is to develop a thorough knowledge through reduction and building up. Reduction is the process of bringing all features and benefits of a product down to the perceptual level, and, in some cases, down to the chemical or molecular level. Building up is the process of invention and innovation.

Today, as society advances, the quality and diversity of products also advances. Companies advance their products and services by engaging in thorough redesigns of their products, services, and business processes. To stay competitive, they need to be constantly seeking improvements and economies that get things done more efficiently as well as reduce production costs which in turn reduce prices.

This is generally called research and development (R&D) and is a critical process for companies that want to stay in business. I have done some work in the "product management" field. I know about the Acceptance Curve and Product Life Cycle, both of which are ways to keep track of the viability of products and to manage company investments in production and returns. As a business professional, I would suggest you research these fields to be able to understand your company better.

However, the development of new ideas can be done by anyone since all thought is individual. It is important to have detailed business process and product knowledge especially the processes that take place before, during and after production.

The key to new ideas is two-fold:

1. Taking next steps.
2. Taking totally new directions.

Taking next steps

Next steps in product development means finding the next available improvement in a product, service, or business process. You learn about this in two ways, 1) by looking at each element of the product, service, or process and, 2) researching if there are new materials, arrangements or steps that will (or might) improve it.

One good way is to read scientific articles and/or papers about the product, service, or business process to see if there have been any new developments in the field. You should also look at scientific research in other fields to see if any of these developments can be applied to your product or service.

For each product, the company should keep a product book (or database) in which you record everything you learn during these studies. This data can be looked at later when it is time to make the next advance.

You can create an SOP (Standard Operating Procedure Manual) for each service and/or business process. These books can provide valuable information that you can take with you into each meeting with associates. They will show how seriously you take the idea of making improvements in your company.

You can also include (in these books) what you have learned about the company's competitors; how they do things, what materials they use and what makes their products, services, or business processes different from yours. This could provide valuable information and keep your company ahead of the curve when it comes to improving and serving the customer better.

Taking Totally New Directions

The premise of this approach is not that you want to improve your existing products and services but that want to invent a new product that better meets the needs of new or existing customers. To explain, let's assume that your company offers gasoline products to customers for use in their cars and other machines. You could say that you are a gasoline company.

But is this true? Aren't you really an energy company since energy is the component of gasoline that the customer uses to improve his life? This broader perspective on your purpose serves the goal of keeping you focused on a broader scale. Consider what would happen if a competitor found a new method or a new product that provided more energy at a lower cost; a product that was not petroleum based but that did the job that petroleum does more efficiently and at a better price. Where would your company be if this happened? Out of business.

To prevent this, your company can take a long-term approach by expanding its vision and be ahead of the game. It can develop other energy products and services that will help you stay viable. You can either beat your competitors to the new approach or you can have other approaches ready to put into action so your company stays viable.

To stay ahead of the curve, you should keep abreast of all new research in the energy field, maybe even hire scientists who can give you an edge in developing new approaches. This will also help you to develop patents that could prevent your competitors from venturing into a new development that you have discovered.

An important key to developing new ideas often involves what I call making new connections. A new connection in this context involves combining products, product goals and/or product characteristics. It could even involve connecting certain business processes in such a way that there is more integration in the company, reduced costs, and increased efficiency (which could reduce prices and make the company more profitable).

As an example of connection of concepts, we could look at electricity. Once it was identified by Franklin, its characteristics could be defined, and those characteristics led to the creation of thousands of life-enhancing products that require electricity for power. In fact, even machines that required human labor as power were converted over and this reduced the human labor involved and significantly increased comfort, ease and productivity of those same men who were no longer using their arms or legs to power these machines. Additionally, electric motors (another connection) could now be used to power carts (once powered by horses and boats once powered by wind).

Another key is the manager's ability to generate and use wide abstractions. An abstraction is an unseen principle that is discovered in nature. Using the example above, "electricity" required a wide abstraction that was not directly observed or understood in nature. Once it was discovered, the wider abstraction of energy conversion led to the understanding of how energy is released in the world and how it can be created or generated to produce more power.

So, the principle of energy conversion of electricity led to the wider principle of energy conversion in the world which put men on the path to discovering even more powerful forms of energy. This led, eventually, to the gasoline powered engine and nuclear energy plants. The limited field of electricity led to the wider abstraction of "methods of energy conversion" and man became even more productive without increasing the level of his manual labor. Instead, he used intellectual labor to design machines that created more energy than thought possible even a few hundred years ago.

These examples are only a few of the basic concepts that have to do with creating new ideas. The key is to connect knowledge to reality and let it help you lighten your labor as well as increase your comfort and leisure. Example: the air conditioner.

How is Your Vocabulary?

Is your vocabulary business-centered and appropriate to the business world in which you operate? Are you often lacking in language skills, unable to express yourself clearly and intelligently? Do people understand you when you speak?

Clear communication in your field is important. You pick this up in college so when you enter the working world, you display your ability to communicate through the "language" of your field.

If you enter the working world without a specific education or experience, you'll need to learn how to communicate with other employees. There is such a thing as business English that represents a general way of showing that you have respect for your bosses and your customers. This not only involves your speech but also your general appearance and personal hygiene. Don't expect to get a job that requires you to be in front of customers if you sport tattoos all over your body and face. Also, be respectful; avoid argumentative behavior around your fellow employees and customers. Show that you possess a modicum of politeness, respect, and good behavior.

If you approach your job with the attitude that others should accommodate your language and vocabulary habits, you will negatively affect your chances of success. It is far better for you to learn the common patterns of speech and vocabulary in a business environment. Not only will it help you deal with your day-to-day issues at work, but it will make you a more valuable employee.

There is no benefit to expecting the world to make your habits normal. It just won't happen unless your habits are already normal. This includes your ability to get along with your fellow employees. This habit of "getting along" makes your life much easier because it establishes common standards that are also accepted by most customers.

Dealing with Conflict at Work

Conflict at work is a very common problem. Sometimes, it proceeds from an employee who does not like his job or who has a bias of some sort. Sometimes, it is the boss who does not like his job or has a bias. It could also be an employee who does not like capitalism or is afraid of the assertive behavior of people who want to succeed. Sometimes it is mere jealousy of successful people and a desire to harm assertive individuals.

It is not good to psychoanalyze people who have bad attitudes about their work and jobs. That type of analysis takes highly specialized skills that most of us do not have, and it would be presumptuous to think that we could do it. The only thing one can do is judge their actions as good or bad for the company by a rational standard. How does one do this?

The rational standard in judging actions in a company are what is the individual doing that is good or bad for the company. Does it harm or help the profit picture, the bottom line? Does it benefit the productive ability of other individuals in the company? Does it harm or help the company's position in the marketplace as a good place to work? These questions and other similar questions can help you determine if an individual is advancing the long-term goals of the company. Decide by means of a careful analysis of these issues and, most often, you will be able to decide whether an individual and his actions and words are good for the company.

A Boss You Do Not Like

Sometimes, we must work with a boss that we don't like. This could be someone we judge to be obnoxious, cruel, impolite, or abusive. You must be careful about judging this individual by a rational standard and avoid judging him or her emotionally or according to wrong standards. You do this by asking some important questions:

1. Does this individual harm or help the profit picture, the bottom line?
2. Does he or she benefit the productive ability of other individuals in the company?

3. Does he or she harm or help the company's position in the marketplace as a good place to work?

If his or her characteristic way of acting does not negatively affect these issues, perhaps you are using an emotional or arbitrary standard when judging.

Other questions you can ask are how does this individual's behavior affect others in the work place and do others have the same view of this individual?

The answers to these questions, if accurately made, can help you decide whether you should stay with this company, seek some sort of redress, or try to work it out with the boss.

I have been in situations where I hated my boss, but I liked the company for which I was working. It was a chore coming to work and many times I hated getting up in the morning because I knew I would have an unpleasant day. In fact, many people in this type of situation may find that in the long run they would be better off by learning to accept the situation and hope for a turn of events that are in their favor.

If, on the other hand, this individual is too intolerable, you must do what you must. I don't believe you have an obligation to save a company from disaster if the management of the company does not understand the company's needs.

How to Get Your Boss on Your Side

Rather than engage in conflict with the boss, how about getting the boss on your side? Given that your boss is a rational person who understands his industry and how to run a successful company; the likelihood is that he will welcome an employee who can give him great efficiencies and more profits and, if he is indeed rational, he will also ensure that you are rewarded for those efforts. Why not, then, enlist him as your mentor who can help you rise with the company and earn more income?

The key is letting your boss know about your

aspirations and the kinds of facts, ideas, and subjects that you need to learn to be a better employee. I learned early in my career that my boss could be my best ally and that he or she was more than willing to help me rise through the steps of the management ladder. If he liked the work I was doing, I knew he would help me in any way he could.

Which brings up the point, how much are you doing creatively to make a difference in the company? Are you innovative, looking for new opportunities, new business process improvements? In short, are you seen as someone who is always pushing the limits and working to make a difference? The more your boss trusts that you are going to do an excellent job, the more he can concentrate on improving the company in other ways.

At UPS, they had a great way of keeping the dialogue among managers going; and that was by having monthly and sometimes weekly one-on-one meetings to see how things were running, what was right, what was wrong and what could be done to make things better. These one-on-one meetings were crucial for letting other managers know that I was in the game and eager to do something to help the company run more smoothly. Such meetings can be career builders for the smart employee. If you don't have such a meeting with your boss, they can be done informally, or you can ask your boss if you can schedule such a meeting on an on-going basis. Regardless of who you are meeting with, it is important that you have something to contribute, that it is relevant and consistent with company values.

These meetings are your best opportunities to communicate your commitment to improve things at the company. Be especially aware of your boss's views on improvement. Is he a boss who thinks that his systems are the best possible? Does he get upset when someone suggests changes? If he does, he might not be open to new ideas and a good heart-to-heart talk about making things better might be out of the question.

Conflict with the Boss

But your boss's attitude toward positive and constructive change is a vital clue about his policies and the prospects for improving things. I once had a boss tell me that my suggestions for improvement indicated a negative attitude. I was shocked that he would think so since my suggestions were intended to help improve a situation that we both thought deficient. Apparently, we had missed communication and I learned later that there were other issues involved. The company didn't last long after I stopped making suggestions and even though my department was the most productive in the company, I was let go. It did show me that the wrong attitude from a boss can destroy a company. Learning how to handle yourself can prove a vital help in your development as a manager.

In those situations, it is important that you be civil; never directly confront the boss especially if he is emotionally tied to "the way things work around here". Always convey a positive attitude and a desire to do the right thing.

Nevertheless, it is important that you and your boss are on the same page; that he knows you are trying to help and that your concern is for positive change that will improve the company's ability to compete in the marketplace. Don't be an "agitator" for the kinds of change that will cost the company lots of money or that have nothing to do with the bottom line. These will often get you labelled as a "disrupter" and get you tossed.

In some companies, there is nothing you can do to improve a negative situation; and you must respect the fact that your company might have been doing business this way for decades – primarily because it was the boss's original idea, and he might never change it; he might even think it is disruptive to modify it. So, always get the lay of the land and learn as much about the reasons why things are done in a particular way. At the very least, it might give you information that you can use in your future career somewhere else or at your own company.

This chapter is about getting the boss on your side and sometimes it is best to let the boss be the boss. Learn from him, respect him and always thank him for the opportunity he has given you. Eventually, you'll know everything he knows and the rest you can figure out.

Gossip

Employees who engage in gossip and innuendo among themselves are not positive influences on the company. They create false impressions and prejudices that do nothing to help the company be successful. It is best not to be involved in such negativity and to avoid it at all costs. If you feel that a particular individual is spreading false rumors or negatively influencing another individual's prospects, there is nothing wrong with refusing to believe such falsehoods; and if they are particularly damaging, there is nothing wrong with discreetly asking the person not to discuss such issues around you. If any such gossip can lead to legal problems for the company, such as a violation of a government regulation, it is important that the management be informed.

Inspiration

I've always gained energy and enthusiasm by reading the works of great men as it came from their own pens or mouths. Such men are your precursors; they created the world from which you draw so much value. They created the world that feeds you, energizes you and inspires you. Here are some quotes I like and some additional thoughts.

1. To finish first, you must first finish. – Juan Manuel Fangio

Never take a leap into the unknown unless you have done everything possible to understand the situation. There is always the option of doing something with more knowledge rather than doing it without knowing what will happen. Life requires risk and many times we don't know what will happen when we take that step or leap. But good skills, eye-to-hand coordination, lots of knowledge and preparation can pull you through. Always be studying your craft, develop new skills when you can and constantly be reading and learning about how the world works. Only the man who takes the motor apart can learn how to make it run faster. And he is the individual who will finish first more often.

2. Nobody remembers the guy who finished second but the guy who finished second. – Bobby Unser

I hate the idea of being known as the guy who finished second. But accomplishment is not about what people think about you; it is about the effort and the desire. Always know how badly you want something and make sure you learn what it will take to win that race.

As a young pitcher, when playing in organized baseball, I accomplished a no-hitter. I will always have it in me that I pitched that no-hitter even though I was playing against average high school level players. There were some pretty good hitters in that league, and I remember studying each one, learning their weaknesses and knowing precisely what I had to do to strike them out. I also did everything I could to make it harder for a hitter to hit my pitches, I studied every possible type of pitch and added it to my repertoire. I practiced throwing to improve my accuracy so I could put the ball exactly where I wanted to. I sought complete control over every pitch I made and developed my skill so I would be effective with every pitch and every move of my body while on the pitcher's mound.

I also knew that being "that good" was also a reflection of how I treated my body; what I ate, how much sleep I got and how much exercise and practice I had undertaken. The morning of my no-hitter I woke up feeling complete, relaxed, competent, good. I told myself that morning that I was feeling better than I had ever felt before and that I could do anything I wanted to accomplish. It was a feeling of total competence, mental, physical, and ideational. When I got on that mound that day, there was total confidence, fearlessness, and complete happiness about who I was and what I was going to do. My precision on that mound was incredible. I could put the ball anywhere I wanted. I could select the best location I wanted, my curveball was perfect as was my slider and knuckleball. Everything worked and I knew I could dominate over every batter. That is what success requires – total commitment and total domination over my actions and choices.

3. Calling upon my years of experience, I froze at the controls. – Stirling Moss

Experience matters. That's why practice is important. That's why testing and study are important. Having known some of the world's great athletes has given me a unique perspective on what success requires. In particular, the race car driver must have total knowledge of his environment, the heat of the day, the heat of the track, how much rubber is on the track, how fast is the wind, which direction is it coming from and where is the sun, etc., etc., etc. But more than this, how well you know that track, where the apex is on every turn, how does the angle of the track affect your car and your ultimate speed, etc. Practice makes a difference and though the track is virtually the same with every lap, there are still variables that you must take into consideration and react to with lightning-like quickness. You must be in supreme physical health, and you must be able to know completely what your car is doing at every instant. Practice and experience makes a difference.

I've noticed that there is a learning curve with every athlete and every type of activity. The first year or two, he is learning the track, his car, his environment and considering every possible variable, what he will do if a car cuts him off, is braking differently or is having trouble staying on the track. As he grows in experience, he learns how to finish first and once he finishes first, he will be able to finish first more often; he will control his variables and influence how the race will proceed. He'll learn how to win before the race is even started, by preparing himself physically, mentally, and strategically. He'll even know how to take charge of his race-strategy and how to run the team, so it runs like a well-oiled machine. His team is as important as his race car; and it is "his" car to know, to study, to feel, to love and to own totally. His car is an extension of his mind and body.

Successful drivers are like engineers, understanding the set ups, recommending minute changes; after all he is the one person who knows the car better than anyone else; he drives it. No one else on the team has that experience so he knows it is up to him to know everything and communicate to the team manager and engineers and strategists exactly what he needs to communicate so they have complete understanding of what he means when he says he wants something.

More than anything, he knows the feel, the smell, the taste, the excitement of victory – a feeling like no other possible. He knows the emotions and thoughts of the primordial hunter who figured out how to kill a large animal, the feelings, and thoughts of the first architect who built his own home with his bare hands, the first business entrepreneur who created the first industry and even the small businessperson who feeds his family with his profits. The victor is the individual who knew everything he needed to know to be the best at doing the hardest. He is, in a sense, the highest intelligence in the freest body. There is nothing like victory at a hard task. Only those who have experienced it can know it. They are the elite of humanity living an existence that few people can understand.

4. I don't know driving in another way which isn't risky. Each one has to improve himself. Each driver has his limit. My limit is a little bit further than other's. - Ayrton Senna

Ayrton Senna was the ultimate driver. He was on the edge of disaster with every second behind the wheel. While he was alive, he was the standard of excellence and very few other drivers could match his perfection.

5. It is amazing how many drivers, even at the Formula One Level, think that the brakes are for slowing the car down. – Mario Andretti

Mario Andretti knew the formula for success. Be the best physically. Drive the best and most advanced car. Strive for perfection with every turn of the wheel. Take risks and never settle for second place.

6. Once you've raced, you never forget it…and you never get over it. - Richard Childress

7. Race cars are neither beautiful nor ugly. They become beautiful when they win. – Enzo Ferrari

8. To achieve anything in this game you must be prepared to dabble in the boundary of disaster. - Sterling Moss

9. What's behind you doesn't matter. – Enzo Ferrari

10. If someone said to me that you can have three wishes, my first would have been to get into racing, my second to be in Formula 1, my third to drive for Ferrari. – Gilles Villeneuve

One thing I've noticed about winners is that they always want the best; and they are usually unsatisfied without it. The best of everything. Everything.

11. The crashes people remember, but drivers remember the near misses. – Mario Andretti

12. Luck is when opportunity meets preparation." - Johnny Rutherford

---

13. "No attack; no chance." – Takuma Sato

14. "Speed costs money. How fast do you want to go?" – Roger Penske

In any great endeavor, there comes a moment when you must act. It is the moment when the victory is made, the moment that all the practice and strategic planning have been about; you know immediately that this – THIS – is the moment that you must grab, hold on to and clutch closely; because it is the moment when VICTORY stands in front of you. This is the moment of opportunity, the moment when danger means nothing, money means nothing, awards and trophies are mere trifles; it is the moment when even death, the end of everything, matters not; THIS is your moment of greatness, and YOU must put everything else aside because you know that you are ready. It is the moment right before you say: "I DID IT!" – Robert Villegas

"Knowledge is Power." – Francis Bacon

Bacon is one of the greatest thinkers in history. This quote is one of the greatest expressions of respect for the ability of human knowledge to help the life of man.

"Nature, to be commanded, must be obeyed." – Francis Bacon

This quote clearly expresses the fact that acknowledging nature, and it's cause and effect, is the means for effecting change and making action meaningful.

Today's failure makes possible tomorrow's success. The most successful men are those who have failed more often than others. They've learned from their mistakes. So, go out there and don't be afraid to make mistakes.

"Wealth does not grow in nature; it has to be produced by men." – Ayn Rand, *The Money-Making Personality*

"Wealth is the product of man's intellect; of his creative activity." – Ayn Rand, *The Money-Making Personality*

"Dress for Success!" – John T. Molloy

"Step up; don't step back." – Robert Villegas

"Your life's purpose is essentially the wider value to which you dedicate your productive work career. When I say "wider value", I mean that your purpose is the one goal that comprises all of your other values."

"This is not to say that your work can't help others (all productive work helps others in trade); but it is to say that your purpose MUST be YOUR purpose; it must enable you to derive a high degree of personal satisfaction without the filter of approval from others." – Robert Villegas, The REAL Purpose-Driven Life

About the Author

Robert Villegas, Jr. is an American Author specializing in business books, fiction, romance, theater, and philosophy. He was born in South Texas (Weslaco) but raised in Indiana. He is Hispanic American but American in every sense of the word. He has spent a lifetime in the business world as a UPS executive and he has also worked in locations all over the United States and Europe. He is an Army veteran who served in Korea as a telecommunications specialist serving in the 7th Infantry Division in Camp Casey, Korea. He was educated in Indiana and earned a Degree through the University of the State of NY (Albany) via an external degree program. He is divorced with three grown children and three grandchildren.

Business Books by Robert Villegas

These four books by Robert Villegas comprise some of the business books that he has written. As an executive working for several companies, he was able to develop these methods that will help anyone seeking to excel in the business world. These books are:

How to Be a Great Employee – and a Greater Manager
You cannot be a great manager without first being a great employee. And this is something that requires learning, experience and attitude. The attitude comes from you but the learning and experience you should acquire through diligent study and practice. http://amzn.to/2BqdG2i $3.99 Kindle $8.95 softcover

SWOT Analysis Supercharged
A SWOT Analysis is an objective look at the internal and external elements of your organization that impact your success or lack thereof. If done diligently, you will always have a handle on what you need to do to improve season after season.
http://amzn.to/2BCAWYx $3.99 Kindle $6.95 softcover

The Five-Module Call Center Training System
The Five-Module Call Center Training System is designed to assist the Call Center Team Leader in helping his employees quickly upgrade their skills to an acceptable level. http://amzn.to/2B3Svj1 $3.99 Kindle $5.95 softcover

Website Development Methodology
Effective strategic marketing requires the ability to differentiate the website development organization and its deliverables from those of the competition. http://amzn.to/2DnYMqh $2.99 Kindle $12.95 softcover

www.robertvillegas.com

Alcoholism and Addiction – the System

These four books comprise a system that can be used by both patients and counselors who are battling Alcoholism and Addiction. Based upon Mr. Villegas's own system developed during his struggle against alcoholism, this system includes:

Alcoholism and Addiction – A Secular Ten-Step Program
This groundbreaking book offers a secular approach to alcoholism unlike that offered by Alcoholics Anonymous. We recommend that every individual going for alcohol and drug-abuse counseling be given a copy of this book which contains the workbook and the two versions of The World's first drunk. http://amzn.to/2md6R9w $3.45 Kindle $11.95 softcover

The Secular Ten-Step Program Workbook
This booklet covers the program developed by Mr. Villegas. It is designed as a workbook with blank spaces for the patient to write his own thoughts as he takes each of the ten steps. Order one copy for each patient in counseling. http://amzn.to/2lrHimS $4.49 Kindle $6.95 softcover

The World's First Drunk – With Counselor Talking Points
This booklet is designed for the counselor as he works with patients during individual or group therapy. It contains helpful tips on discussing the life story of the man who invented alcohol. Order one copy for each patient in counseling. http://amzn.to/2l446Wr $2.99 Kindle $5.95 softcover

The World's First Drunk – Patient Version
This version of the short story contains empty spaces where the patient can answer questions about the life story of the man who invented alcohol. Order one copy for each counselor. http://amzn.to/2ldxBGb $2.99 Kindle $5.95 softcover.

www.robertvillegas.com

Books on Religion

The Mark of Titus
Excerpts from the book Unkilling Jesus which highlight some of the key discoveries implied by new theories about the origin of the Jesus Myth. The idea that the Romans invented Christianity is the basic premise of new theories about the origin of Christianity.http://amzn.to/2itMCo0 $3.49 Kindle $5.95 softcover

Contra Religion
This book is designed as a "shorter" explanation of the ideas presented in my larger book, "Behind the Ritual Mask" which seeks to define fundamental principles of religion. I'm hoping this book will serve as a primer for the original book and spur an interest in reading it. http://amzn.to/2yWMSlx $3.99 Kindle $6.95 softcover

Is this the Face that Launched a Thousand Ships?
It was love at first sight. I saw her one day while watching a television program about King Tut, whose tomb had been discovered by Howard Carter years before. I was looking at the famous bust of a beautiful Egyptian Queen. https://amzn.to/3t487x3 $3.99 Kindle $7.95 softcover

The History of Altruism
The History of Altruism is a historical treatment of the development of altruism throughout time from the Paleolithic period to today. It tracks the development of self-sacrifice of primitive man to the advent of altruism as a development from Kant's "duty". It covers a broad sweep of concepts and shows how they influenced modern man, religion and societies through the ages. https://amzn.to/3gN8zgy $4.19 Kindle 14.95 paperback.

www.robertvillegas.com

Books on Christianity

Unkilling Jesus
Who was Paul and what was his role in the creation of Christianity? What was his provenance, and did he meet the resurrected Christ? Who wrote Revelation and what was the document's purpose? Why was Domitian assassinated? http://amzn.to/2itMCoO $3.99 Kindle $15.95 softcover

Domitian: The Final Messiah
The central goal of this book is to define the specific themes and concepts that make up Domitian's contribution to Christianity – in a sense, we are defining the specific Domitian overlay to the Christian materials originally developed for Titus. http://amzn.to/2yWMSlx $2.99 Kindle $6.95 softcover

Paul's Agon and the Mystification of History
Paul and Jesus are joined in one important way; the way of a miracle. They met on the road to Damascus while Paul supposedly pursued Christians. Jesus, in a sense, told Paul to get with the program and stop persecuting his people. In this incident, the Bible tells us that Jesus is already dead, and resurrected. This book argues otherwise. http://amzn.to/2zSDsuP $5.99 Kindle $19.95 softcover

Christianity on the Arch of Titus
This book explores the "persons" visible on the Triumphant Arch of Titus which is located in the heart of Rome. These people were significant in that they played a role, not only in Rome's conquest of Judaea but also in the creation of Christianity. This book explores those individuals and the roles they played in the creation of one of the most important religious movements in world history. https://amzn.to/3xz3OgM $3.69 Kindle 10.95 paperback.

www.robertvillegas.com

Values and Purpose Books by Robert Villegas

The Real Purpose-Driven Life
After centuries of being told that it is not about you, it is time to set the record straight. You are a unique individual and your goal in life should be to achieve your own happiness. This book is about helping you accomplish your goals and fixing your purpose firmly in place. It covers not only why you should pursue your goals but how to do it. https://amzn.to/3ebkhjr $3.99 Kindle $6.95 softcover

The Values and Purpose Workbook
Rather than give you tasks that involve doing a lot of things for other people, I'm am going to tell you that focusing on yourself will reveal your life's purpose and express your passions and freedom. I'm going to start with you. https://amzn.to/3eQf4wG $2.99 Kindle $6.95 softcover

This Book is About You
Some people move briskly bent on a purpose, concerned only about what they are about. People walk by them; they don't even notice. They just keep to their path and you wonder where they are going. This book is about you. It's about time. https://amzn.to/3vFMzss $6299 Kindle $5.95 softcover

www.robertvillegas.com

Self-Help Books by Robert Villegas

Existence a Rational Thoughtbook
A Rational Thoughtbook is designed for thinking as opposed to reading. It combines brief prescient content with stunning imagery. Existence focuses on the nature of existence and gives you intelligent thoughts to integrate into your life.
https://amzn.to/2RZpsKV $4.99 Kindle $12.95 softcover

The Virtue of Independence
One of the most important goals for any person is to establish intellectual independence. Intellectual independence is the road to "life" independence, which is the ability to earn your own way without help from others. https://amzn.to/3awuCV2 $2.99 Kindle $6.95 softcover

Rational Meditation
Rational Meditation is self-meditation. It is thinking about yourself without guilt and without the tenets of modern philosophy (that the world is unknowable, that man is a phony, that ethics and living are only about others). https://amzn.to/3gus9OE $6.99 Kindle $12.95 softcover

History of My Mind
This booklet is the companion to my book entitled Rational Meditation. It utilizes the various exercises of the original book that involve contemplation or meditation and provide space for written input by the reader. https://amzn.to/3gy3hpl $4.69 Kindle $11.95 softcover.

www.robertvillegas.com

Rational Thoughtbooks by Robert Villegas

Existence a Rational Thoughtbook
A Rational Thoughtbook is designed for thinking as opposed to reading. It combines brief prescient content with stunning imagery. Existence focuses on the nature of existence and gives you intelligent thoughts to integrate into your life.
https://amzn.to/2RZpsKV $4.99 Kindle $12.95 softcover

Identity
One of the most important goals for any person is to establish intellectual independence. Intellectual independence is the road to "life" independence, which is the ability to earn your own way without help from others. https://amzn.to/3nf9aJn $3.99 Kindle $9.95 softcover

www.robertvillegas.com

Fiction and Creative Poems and Plays

Poetic Prose and Poetry
These expressions represent some of Mr. Villegas' deepest thoughts as he lived and traveled throughout the world in locations such as Germany (East and West), Austria, Britain, Spain, Canada, France, Luxembourg, Belgium, the Netherlands, Korea, New York, Miami, San Francisco and other locations. https://amzn.to/3vu7X3B $2.99 Kindle $6.95 softcover

The Lost Poems
These poems were discovered among Mr. Villegas's archives in 2016. Many of them have been read by only Mr. Villegas. Most of these poems were rejected as "not that good". After seeing them again, he has changed his mind. These poems expressive, fresh and spontaneously honest.
https://amzn.to/3aPg5nB $3.99 Kindle $6.95 softcover

Adam Reborn – A Short Play
Adam Reborn is a play of symbols. Adam and Eve, as I have portrayed them, are young and heroic people learning to deal with a Paradise and God that are hostile to them. There is no chance of life for them.
https://amzn.to/3u9Nr8b $2.99 Kindle $6.95 softcover

The Boy Who Stood Alone
Jonny Payne has just discovered Ayn Rand and his parents don't know what to do. They take him to a priest and a psychologist but his only question is "What is the price of independence? https://amzn.to/3nCG6ve $3.99 Kindle $6.95 paperback.

www.robertvillegas.com

Fiction and Creative Materials

Aphrodite
Johnny is a Spanish guitar player with a mysterious past. At a party, he meets the beautiful songstress Aphrodite who is enthralled with his flamenco guitar skills. Later, she learns they have a connection, a particular song they both appear to know. Aphrodite discovers the connection, and through dreams, the two fall in love. The question is whether they will ever be together. https://amzn.to/3xIlmXZ $3.99 Kindle $5.95 softcover

The Odyssey of Amerigo the Founder
Amerigo was born in a time of desperation and dystopia. He was the only man with the vision of a great future. Many repaired to his cause while others swore to destroy him. They wanted his life, his mind and everything he loved. He swore that no matter what they did, he would win the struggle for freedom and a new future. https://amzn.to/2Qz8h2t $3.99 Kindle $8.95 softcover

Bob and Bobbie
1967 - a town outside Camp Casey, Korea - two young people have come together to challenge a world that makes love impossible. https://amzn.to/3sZWSpf $2.99 Kindle $5.95 softcover

The Raven Haired Girl
Bobby met Angie 52 years ago in a poor neighborhood in Indianapolis. It was love at first sight. For a few short months, their relationship blossomed into love. They were in love but didn't know how to be in love because they were only fourteen years old. https://amzn.to/3306plF $2.99 Kindle $6.95 paperback.

www.robertvillegas.com

Other Books by Robert Villegas

 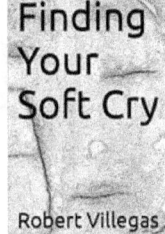  

Naming Names in the NT
"Discovery consists of seeing what everybody has seen and thinking what nobody has thought." - Albert Szent-Gyogyi – 1937 Nobel Laureate
https://amzn.to/3mXR66H $3.99 Kindle $9.95 softcover $16.95 hardcover

Finding Your Soft Cry
Every individual has a yearning to know that he is both free and good. This yearning comes to him from early youth, and he hopes that he eventually develops the intellectual tools to help him distinguish between his nature and the demands of society. The key to freedom is the ability to act without restriction and, especially, without guilt. https://amzn.to/3p8lY7m $3.99 Kindle $8.95 softcover $15.95 hardcover

The New Totalitarianism – Quo Vadis?
The previous century was one of the bloodiest in history. Two World Wars and many other wars do not bode well for our century that is beginning to rival the previous in its bloodlust. If we look carefully, we find in the last century the philosophical roots of the present century. The philosophers of the last century are the philosophers of the present. https://amzn.to/3AMZNFC $5.99 Kinde $10.95 softcover $25.95 hard cover

A Call to Reason
Is it possible that the problems in the world are not caused by capitalism and rich people? Is it possible that anti-capitalism and anti-reason philosophies are nothing more than elaborate hoaxes designed to convince people to give up everything they have honestly earned and take it away from them? Is it possible they are caused by the re-distribution of capital to wasteful uses and the consequent destruction of jobs and affluence? https://amzn.to/3mVNrq5 $5.99 Kindle $9.95 softcover $24.95 Hardcover

www.robertvillegas.com

Poems for the Stage

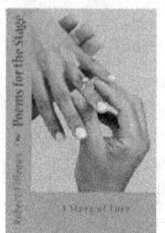 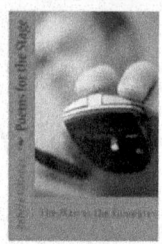

Poems for the Stage – A Story of Love
This dramatic presentation features poems found in Mr. Villegas's book Poetic Prose and Poetry. Some are also found in his book.
https://amzn.to/3gSJctV $2.99 Kindle $5.95 softcover

Poems for the Stage – The Man at the Computer
This dramatic presentation is based upon poems from Mr. Villegas's book Poetic Prose and Poetry. Some of the poems have been slightly altered to reflect the internal story. Mr. Villegas's book Poetic Prose and Poetry can be found on Amazon.com.
https://amzn.to/2R8zpFf $2.99 Kindle $5.95 softcover

www.robertvillegas.com

More Books on Politics and History

A Boomer takes on the Far Left
I just learned something about myself – and it isn't very good. In fact, it is very bad. I learned that the opinions of Boomers don't matter any more. We are obsolete in this new age of new knowledge. Anything we think is unimportant and false. I don't think so. https://amzn.to/3tzNqtc $5.19 Kindle $10.95 softcover

Crushing the Alinsky Radicals
The worst enemy of individual rights today is a group of people I call the Alinsky Radicals. These people are now in charge of our culture and temporarily, in charge of government. They are associated, philosophically and politically, with the communists and fascists of the past. They are not your father's liberals. They are the direct descendants of dictators such as Stalin and Mao. In this book, I hope to convince you of the evil of the Alinsky Radicals and to provide the intellectual ammunition you need to eradicate them from society.
https://amzn.to/3hbh9WN $3.49 Kindle $8.95 softcover

The Conservative's Dilemma
I wrote this book to ask some important questions about the conservative philosophy of altruism. https://amzn.to/3bfDQ8e $2.99 Kinde $6.95 softcover.

The Biggest Mistakes in History – 2008 to 2016
To be the Chief Executive of the greatest country in the world requires a leader with a great deal of knowledge, experience and reasoning ability. It requires having the very best minds as advisors, minds that the President can count on to give reasoned arguments and detailed knowledge about the important issues of the day. I think it takes a special ability to understand the principle of cause and effect concerning how government action impacts the lives of real people.
https://amzn.to/3tDQ4Ol $2.99 Kindle $10.95 softcover

www.robertvillegas.com

Books on Politics and History

Dachau and Berlin in 1990
This booklet chronicles Mr. Villegas' thoughts during visits to Dachau and Berlin during 1990, disclosing my observations of milestones in German history, past and present, and relating those events to world happenings as they were unfolding at the time. I traveled throughout Germany for much of 1990 while on business. https://amzn.to/3ex578d $2.99 Kindle $6.95 softcover

What Harvard and Princeton Don't Want You to Know
The professors at Harvard and Princeton don't want you to know about the worst ideas in history. This is because they have been pawning these ideas off as true and profound. They have been using them to deceive and manipulate us for centuries. https://amzn.to/3farP5p $5.19 Kindle $9.95 softcover

Defending American Values
This book is made up of several chapters about American values and how they can be defended without a descent into the abyss of dictatorship. The book argues for individual rights and provides reasons why we should fight for them. https://amzn.to/3uMFq9L $3.99 Kinde $5.95 softcover.

Capitalism Doesn't Fail
How many times have we heard the old saw: "Capitalism has failed again" over the course of contemporary events? We heard it during the Great Depression of 1929 after Hoover had invoked tariffs and precipitated economic retaliation and a banking crisis. Along with this question usually came a statement to the effect, that "We can fix capitalism and make it even stronger by issuing economic controls or spending money to stimulate economic activity." This book will argue that capitalism, as an economic system, cannot fail as long as individuals are free to act. https://amzn.to/3xZIAJ6 $4.19 Kindle $10.95 softcover

www.robertvillegas.com

Books on Psychology and Virtue

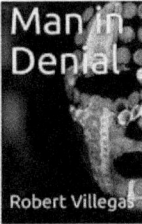   

Man in Denial
If psychology has no solid epistemology and metaphysics, how can it stand on its own? I do not think it can and this explains why psychology is in such a sad state today. Yet, before we can put psychology on a solid foundation, philosophy too must advance above the level of puberty. With its base in modern philosophy, even philosophy cannot stand on its own which exposes the real problems with modern psychology. https://amzn.to/3oVTDAQ $5.99 Kindle $9.95 softcover $18.95 hardcover

Understanding the Modern Mind
The purpose of this book is to delve into critical issues about how the human mind has come to the modern position of doubt and despair. The culprits in this matter include the irrationality of both rationalism and skepticism, and, in particular, the child of skepticism known as pragmatism.
https://amzn.to/3mRLZF9 $6.99 Kindle $9.60 softcover $26.95 hardcover

How Marcuse Destroyed Capitalism
One of the fathers of critical theory was Herbert Marcuse who escaped European dictatorship only by coming to America. America gave him the freedom and protection he needed to destroy capitalism in America.
https://amzn.to/2YW9LaS $4.99 Kinde $8.95 softcover.

The Logical Fallacy of Altruism
A logical fallacy is a faulty thought process that violates a rule of proper thinking. Correct arguments are defined as proper generalized expressions that define logical truths or knowledge. In effect, a rule of logical reasoning addresses all of the common modes of valid argument while the faulty argument contradicts them. This book examines altruism as a logical fallacy.
https://amzn.to/3vdFiB0 $5.99 Kindle $9.95 softcover $18.95 Hardcover

www.robertvillegas.com

Books on Sport and Entertainment Sponsorship

Finding Sponsors 1 and 2
This book is written for anyone seeking sponsorship relationships in the sport and entertainment fields. The ideas and principles presented here are applicable to any company, sport team, entertainment company, marketing agency and charitable organization that uses corporate sponsorships to support its activities. Volume 1: https://amzn.to/3ejm1Hp $5.19 Kindle $12.95 softcover Volume 2: https://amzn.to/3eVDo0e $4.69 Kindle $10.95 softcover

How to Write a Sponsorship Proposal
This booklet provide you with some basic guidelines on what to communicate in order to produce a winning sponsorship proposal. These guidelines will focus on what you should be presenting to your potential sponsor to make the best business case for involvement with your team or entertainment company. $2.99 Kindle $6.95 softcover

Hospitality Event Planning Handbook
One key part of your sponsorship activation strategy might be customer hospitality events in conjunction with sporting events. How do you pull off a Hospitality Event for your biggest customers? You may not know how to start, what to do and how to ensure the event is a success. This book can help. http://amzn.to/2mxzpgy $7.95 softcover.

Selling Sponsorship in the Age of the Coronavirus
This book provides suggestions on how sport teams, athletes and concert promoters can mitigate the damage done to their businesses by the economic lockdowns (due to the Coronavirus). It integrates checklists, SWOT Analysis and other valuable business aids into one toolkit that will help you keep your sport and/or genre alive in these difficult times. https://amzn.to/2QVBNiM $5.15 Kindle $5.95 softcover

www.robertvillegas.com

Books on Sponsorship and Business

Finding Sponsors Forms Book
This "Forms Book" is intended to provide samples of the forms mentioned in my book "Finding Sponsors for Sport and Entertainment". This will make it possible for you to reproduce these forms in other formats as well as download the forms document from the SponsorProAZ website for use with Microsoft Word.
https://amzn.to/3b95yDW $2.99 Kindle $5.50 softcover

Submitting Your Sponsorship Proposal Online
This booklet enables sport teams and concert promoters to submit their sponsorship proposals to companies that accept only online submission of proposals. https://amzn.to/3euzdti $2.99 Kindle $5.95 softcover

The Art of Sponsorship
This short book is based upon Mr. Villegas' book "Finding Sponsors for Sport and Entertainment". It is also based upon a course that he taught for an organization managing Indiana Parks and Recreation facilities. It is, in a sense, a condensation of information from the book geared toward organizations that would like to earn revenues on their facilities through corporate sponsorship.
https://amzn.to/3beuVnC $2.99 Kinde $6.95 softcover.

Restarting Your Business After the Pandemic
This new book is designed to help you restart your business after the Coronavirus pandemic. You will find here all the right questions, how you can find the answers and the forms you need to walk through your restart and coming success. https://amzn.to/2QVBNiM $5.15 Kindle $5.95 softcover

www.robertvillegas.com

www.ingramcontent.com/pod-product-compliance
Lightning Source LLC
Chambersburg PA
CBHW050216230526
45470CB00001B/416